THE MOST Wonderful TIME OF THE YEAR

Uncommon Lessons
From The Christmas Story

JESSE DUPLANTIS

Published by Harrison House Publishers

Shippensburg, PA 17257

ISBN 13 TP: 978-1-6803-1511-0

ISBN 13 eBook: 978-1-6803-1510-3

ISBN 13 HC: 978-1-6803-1509-7

ISBN 13 LP: 978-1-6803-1511-0

For Worldwide Distribution, Printed in the U.S.A.

2 3 4 5 6 7 8 / 24 23 22 21 20

Contents

Introduction. 9

SECTION ONE:

Caesar Augustus—
The Unconscious Obedience of an Unbeliever 13

Chapter 1: When God Says Something Is Going to Happen, It's
Going to Happen, No Matter What!. 15

Chapter 2: God's Work Doesn't Appeal to Our Senses: It's Not
Always Comfortable, But It Is Always Best. 25

Chapter 3: No Work of God Is Devoid of Power, His Promises Will
Always Come to Pass. 45

Chapter 4: Caesar Wanted to Meet the Needs of a Government, Jesus
Came to Meet the Needs of the People. 55

SECTION TWO:

**John the Baptist—
God Always Sends a Forerunner** **65**

Chapter 5:   John the Baptist—
The Forerunner to Jesus' First Coming 67

Chapter 6:   What Made John Great in God's Sight Will Make You
Great in His Sight, Too 75

Chapter 7:   The Power of Spiritual Preparation 85

Chapter 8:   You Can't Live Two Lives Any More Than You Can Serve
Two Masters 93

SECTION THREE:

**The Wise Men—
When Science and Spirituality Converge:
The Humble and Generous Magi** **101**

Chapter 9:   Scientists, Worshippers, and Givers—The Wise Men
Came with Their Best Intentions and Best Gifts 103

Chapter 10:   Three Rich Gentiles Came to Worship and Give:
Why Do We Fixate on the Manger's Hay? 113

Chapter 11:   The Simple Faith, Undoubting Obedience, and Deep,
Loving Reverence of the Magi. .121

Chapter 12:   Nothing Could Stop the Magi,
Don't Let Anything Stop You 127

SECTION FOUR:

**Mary, Mother of Jesus—
The Favored, the Blessed, the One God Chose to Raise
His Only Son, Jesus.** **137**

Chapter 13:   Mary, the Controversial 139

Chapter 14:   A Divine Support System: The Sacred Bond of Two
Women and Two Babies 151

Chapter 15:   Where Eve Failed, Mary Succeeded: She Kept the Faith...
and Her Divine Secret 157

Chapter 16:   Should We Pray to Mary? And if Not, Why? Should We
Honor Her or Not? 163

SECTION FIVE:

**Jesus—
The Light of the World, the Hope of the Future...
His Story Isn't Finished Yet** **177**

Chapter 17:   The Miracle of Jesus Christ—Baby in the Manger,
God in the Flesh 179

Chapter 18:   Jesus—The Inspiration and Illumination of Our Very
Existence 191

Chapter 19:   The Growing Pains of Christ and Christmas. 203

Chapter 20:   Jesus—He's for Us, in Us, and Working Through Us
Around the World 213

                Salvation Prayer 229

                More About the Author 231

Introduction

I did something crazy. I decided to go to the mall on Black Friday. Let me tell you something…that is one big mistake. Black Friday, the day after the Thanksgiving holiday, seems to be the real kick off of the holiday season for *everybody* in America. So, when my wife, Cathy, said she needed to make a return at the mall, I decided to go, too. I like seeing all the holiday decorations. It puts me in the Christmas spirit.

One of the problems about deciding to go to the mall at Christmastime is that the whole town seems to have the same idea. The place is packed, the sales are running, and the place borders on mass hysteria. You'd think the craziness would hit you at the front doors, but it all starts in the parking lot. Nobody is happy in the mall parking lot at Christmas! Nobody is feeling joyful or generous there. Oh, they might be full of the Christmas spirit two seconds before they pull into the mall parking lot, but all of that goodness goes out the window once they circle the lot for thirty minutes and find nowhere to park.

Now, everywhere I go I find favor. It makes some people mad, but not me! So, I dropped Cathy off at the entrance door and I started circling with the rest of them. I noticed that everybody was tense. Some were even arguing in their car. Others were just beelining around the lot as fast as they could, like hawks coming in for the kill. I didn't want to waste all day doing this, so I prayed aloud, "Jesus, help me!" And right then, a car pulled out of a spot right in front of me. I pulled in and, I swear, I saw people looking at me like they wanted to commit King Herod-style Christmas murder. One guy even cussed right in his car. I couldn't hear him, but I know a cuss word when I see it mouthed at me.

People sure were hot and bothered that day, but not me. There is something to be said for being in the right place at the right time— and even more to be said for walking in the favor of God.

So, I got into that mall and started walking to find my wife and, as I moved through the crowds, I started noticing that everybody seemed to be happy. Whatever devil from hell was hanging out in the parking lot, well, he hadn't made it to the inside of the mall yet. I noticed that everywhere I walked, I saw pretty decorations, buzzing joyful people, and a lot of smiles. Hopefulness, even. It got me thinking about how Christmas changes the atmosphere—and not just in shops, but just about everywhere else, too.

There is an energy in the air that feels just wonderful at Christmas, and I don't think it's about the gifts. I believe it's because, underneath all of that gift buying and buzzing, around, everyone is being affected by the *reason* behind the holiday—Jesus, the Light of the World.

As a believer, I know that there are others like me who are reflecting on Christ as they go about their shopping. I believe that all around the world, people are affected by that baby in a manger so long ago. Joy, peace, love, and good will to all men is a concept that even unbelievers want to experience, I believe, and together we stir up the sweetness in people and we all start seeing the goodness in each other.

That day at the mall, they were playing that old, familiar Christmas song, "It's the Most Wonderful Time of the Year," like they do every year, and as I heard it, I thought, *It is…it really is wonderful*, and I began to think about sharing a message with that title. It turned out to be five messages, and now this book.

I'm not going to just retell you the traditional Christmas story in this book. You already know that. I'm going to share what came up for me as I read through the old, familiar story—what the Holy Spirit showed me that I hadn't really seen before, as well as some teaching that I think can help us in today's world, too.

There are five sections in this book and each focuses on a central person or group from this special time in our history: Caesar Augustus, John the Baptist, the Wise Men, Mary, and Jesus. I hope that as you read the lessons and thoughts that came to my heart, you'll be inspired to see the manger scene that is so common everywhere during this holiday in a fresh way. Who knows? Maybe it'll even help you to get through the mall parking lot a little easier—with more joyful and hopeful thoughts on your mind than just nabbing that holy-grail spot right by the big front doors!

Merry Christmas,
Jesse Duplantis

Caesar Augustus

THE UNCONSCIOUS OBEDIENCE OF AN UNBELIEVER

Chapter 1

When God Says Something Is Going to Happen, *It's Going to Happen, No Matter What!*

Mary was pregnant and not just a little bit. She was heavy with child and at the end of her pregnancy—and like any woman about to give birth, she probably wasn't all that excited to travel far from home. What woman who is near the end of her term *wants* to get on the back of a donkey and travel near a hundred miles? Not many, if any, I'll tell you that much!

If Jesus had been any other baby, He would have likely been born in His own hometown of Nazareth because that's where Joseph and Mary were living. Nazareth, in a region of Israel called Galilee, is where Jesus would eventually be raised and also where His ministry much later would begin. But, in the Christmas story, Jesus fulfills a prophecy when His parents suddenly find themselves on a journey they never really wanted to take.

Now, I'm not going to tell you the whole Christmas story. That's not really what this book is about. But hear me out, because there are some lessons in the Christmas story that I believe will bless you and help you to see the wonderful and unusual way God works.

As I mentioned, it had been prophesied many, many years before that the Anointed One, the Messiah, would be born in Bethlehem—but of course, like many prophecies that seem to take a while to come to pass, people tend to go back to everyday living without an urgency to continue looking for the signs. Before Jesus was born, many babies had been born in the town of Bethlehem—and those babies had grown up, gotten married, and had many babies of their own. So, to the locals, being born in Bethlehem was not considered an automatic blessing or much of a big deal at all, and the same was true for being raised in a city like Nazareth.

So, why *did* Joseph and Mary leave home? Why on earth would Mary get on the back of a donkey and head down south with Joseph to Bethlehem? Why would they do such a thing when they both knew it was inevitable that Mary would soon give birth to Jesus?

There was only *one* reason they left Nazareth—and his name was Caesar Augustus. Caesar was one of the most powerful men in the world at that time, and when he said "move," people had to listen or suffer the consequences. So, while Mary might have been carrying the Savior of the world in her belly and probably wished for the easiest and best delivery of her baby in her hometown, God had other plans.

Caesar didn't know or care about Mary or Joseph at all. In fact, Caesar Augustus had only *one* thing on his mind at the time, and that one thing would be the catalyst for getting Joseph and Mary out of Nazareth so that Jesus could fulfill an old, old prophecy about

Bethlehem. What was on Caesar's mind? The same thing that's on a lot of leaders' minds these days—*taxes!*

CAESAR AUGUSTUS HAD MONEY ON HIS MIND

Everybody wants a piece of the action. Just because Jesus was born over 2,000 years ago doesn't mean that human nature has changed—because as long as there have been leaders ruling people, there have been leaders trying to figure out how to get more money to do the job.

Caesar Augustus had money on his mind. He sent word throughout Israel that it was time for a new census so that he could more accurately tax the working people. Caesar didn't want anybody slipping through the cracks. He wanted more money, and he wanted it quick.

Not only did Caesar want more tax money, he didn't want the government to have to go and find out just how many people were going to need to pay up. He didn't want to send out people to jot down everybody's name—no, Caesar wanted the head of every household to leave home and travel, according to their lineage, to the place where their own ancestral records were kept. Can you guess the town where Joseph's ancestral records were kept? You got it. *Bethlehem.*

Joseph was of the lineage and house of King David, so he had no other choice but to do what Caesar said and go to "the city of David," which is called Bethlehem even to this day. Can you imagine what Mary might have felt when Joseph told her this? Do you think either of them were happy and jumping for joy at the thought of it? Just like nobody really *wants* to pay more taxes, nobody really *wants* to make a tough journey while pregnant. Mary's hormones were probably kicking just like the baby in her belly, and her nesting instincts were probably kicked up high too, and so I imagine she just wanted to stay home—and the truth is, she could have done just that.

Mary didn't have to go to Bethlehem. Only Joseph, as the head of his house, was required to make that journey. Mary *wanted* to go. Why? Well, you have to remember that Joseph was still keeping her away because of the flapping jaws of the people around town. Few believed her story—that an angel had come to her, spoke to her, and caused her virgin womb to quicken with a divine child that she was instructed to call "Jesus." An angel had visited Joseph too, who confirmed the miracle conception, and so he believed and was her greatest ally. And because he loved Mary so much, he chose to isolate her from the community so that she would be able to avoid the humiliation of being seen as her belly grew larger.

Mary relied upon Joseph in many ways. They were in that miraculous predicament together. So I imagine that when Mary heard about the census and knew that Joe had to go, she probably said what any other first-time pregnant mamas would in that moment: "You're not going without *me!*"

What's the moral of all this? God knows what it takes to get people to move where they need to be in life to fulfill His plan—and sometimes what it takes is a little discomfort and a whole lot of obedience and faith. If Nazareth was the "comfort zone" for Joseph and Mary, then Bethlehem was the "discomfort zone"! Yet Bethlehem was exactly where God needed to get them in order to fulfill His plan.

God Knows
What Moves People

God knows the heart of each of us. He knows how we think, and He's not above setting the stage for our eventual success by making us a little uncomfortable in the present. Whatever God calls us to do will require that we need His help—and sometimes His help is a nudge that doesn't feel too comfortable, but it will stimulate us to move forward in His plan for our lives.

God knew what it would take to move Joseph. Joseph was an honorable man who worked as a stonemason carpenter, and he knew that if he and Mary were going to start their lives out right as a family, well, they needed to obey the law of the land. They needed to comply with the decree Caesar ordered and be counted in order that they pay their taxes correctly. God knew Joseph and how Joseph's mind would guide his decisions.

God also knew what it would take to move Mary. She was a pure-hearted woman who trusted God and the desire to be with Joseph, no matter what, was something that was deep in her heart. Mary wanted to have Joseph by her side. If she didn't care, she would have stayed home. Mary wanted his love and support at the birth of their first and God's only Son—and even if following Joseph meant great discomfort for herself, God knew that Mary would choose that path. God knew Mary and how Mary's heart would guide her decisions.

What about Caesar Augustus? What I'd like you to notice now is something hardly anybody mentions when they tell the Christmas story, and it is this: If Caesar was the reason Jesus was born in Bethlehem, then Caesar was the reason the prophecy was fulfilled—and this means that Caesar was moved to action by God, even though Caesar didn't know God at all. Think about that!

Caesar was a heathen—and yet Caesar was the catalyst. Caesar didn't know God—and yet God knew Caesar. Caesar didn't care about the Jewish prophecy or Messiah or anything of the sort—and yet God cared very much about all those things and used an unbelieving man to set things in motion so that His plan for mankind could be done.

Did Caesar even know what was going on? No, he didn't realize God was using him at all. This is what I call "the unconscious obedience of the unbeliever," and it is flat amazing!

EMPERORS ARE BUT OFFICIALS IN GOD'S PLANS

Does God only use believers? No. Sometimes God has to move upon a heathen to get believers to move. Sometimes God has to use an unbeliever to do something a Christian won't do. And whether we like it or not, God often uses people we would never choose.

Emperors are but officials in God's plans. So many people are worried about the state of leadership in America today. So many are worried about the division among the people. The believers are even not often on the same page. Who knows what man or woman God will use? Sometimes only God Himself.

God knows what He is going to do to make certain everything is fulfilled in His Word—and if you think He's going to limit Himself to just using the Church, you are living in a dream world. God is going to use the unconscious obedience of unbelievers to get His Word done, too.

God may put people in office you never thought He would. You don't have to approve or disapprove of God's choices—and to even put ourselves in the spot of judging God for anything is foolish at best. I like to say that arguing with God is like a gnat biting the toe of an elephant—it's irrelevant and doesn't change where the elephant is going to walk next!

Maybe God places one man or woman in office because they are willing to obey His guiding—even when they don't realize Who is nudging them to do X, Y, or Z. Maybe God even uses their bad qualities to facilitate the conditions needed to get God's people to move. Caesar Augustus is proof of that because he knew *nothing* about the Messiah, and he couldn't have cared less about Judea or Jerusalem. All he wanted was tax money, and it's unlikely that he wanted it for something good. It's not like Caesar Augustus was known far and wide for being some wonderful and generous benefactor of the people. Yet God used Caesar's greed anyway to facilitate the fulfillment of prophecy.

You've got to understand something. If you worry a lot over political leaders just remember that no matter what they do, they cannot subvert God's plan in the end—they may hinder it, but they cannot stop it. God can also use anyone He likes and order events the way He sees fit. We don't have to like it. In all truth, we may never understand some of His reasons until we cross over and are no longer looking through a glass darkly—but we can trust that God will see to it that His plan is done.

GOD CAN USE ANYONE—EVEN THOSE WE DON'T LIKE!

I often say that some people aren't "thorns in flesh," to quote a phrase used by Paul the apostle—they are complete bushes! There are some seriously irritating people in this world. Guess what? God still loves them, and God may still use them. So don't discount them just because you don't like them very much. God didn't call us to like people. He called us to love people—and sometimes, we love them from afar! And, sometimes, we simply have to look at our own heart to see just why they trigger our emotions so much. We can learn a lot about ourselves just by seeing what irritates the fire out of us!

Until we get to Heaven and meet our Maker face to face, the truth is that we may never understand why certain emperors, presidents, prime ministers, or kings are in place—and we may not grasp how God can *possibly* use them as officials in His plans for mankind. Not everyone God uses is holy and the epitome of perfection. The truth is that God will use anybody who accepts the nudging of His Spirit—even when they don't realize they are being nudged at all!

Would we prefer all of our leaders to be saved and pious, perfect and holy before God? Absolutely! Sure! But you and I both know that even the ones who *are* saved are not always doing the right things 24/7—and yet there they are, earning both praise and disgust, depending on who's doing the scrutinizing. Another reality of our God is that He gives politicians just as much grace and mercy as He gives any other human being, because unlike human beings, God is not moved by public opinion.

Proverbs 21:1 reads, *"The king's heart is in the hand of the LORD, as the rivers of water: He turneth it whithersoever He will."* In Old Testament times, God used Cyrus to get the Jews back to their homeland too, and Cyrus was not a man of God. Cyrus couldn't have cared less about anything other than what was good for him—but God used his unconscious obedience to bring the Jews back to their homeland. In New Testament times, God used Caesar Augustus to get Jesus where He needed to be, even though all Caesar really cared about was taxes. God can use rulers today too, to move His plan along—don't forget it. It's a crazy thing when you look back sometimes at your own life and realize you should maybe say thanks to a heathen for getting the will of God done!

So, whenever I feel irritated by a president or some other leader, I remember after I get my aggravation in check that emperors are but officials in God's plans. Sometimes to get us to where we ought to be, it takes a good ole heathen unconsciously obeying God! Just like Joseph and Mary, it took Caesar Augustus' greed to make them go in the direction God wanted.

Joseph and Mary didn't have it easy, and I'll get more to them later, but remember that even when they went to Bethlehem there were points along the way that they likely questioned God. Can you imagine knowing your unborn baby came into existence by the hand of God? Can you imagine knowing that the child is so important that angels are sent to you to tell you that fact? You'd think the birth plan would be easy then, right? You'd think there'd be no trouble—God's Son is coming, who can stand against God?

Plenty of people will stand against God, but God can still use them. It's very possible Satan tried to stop Jesus from being born where He should. Was it God's will for there to be no room at the inn? Was it Satan's attempt to hinder God's plan that there was no room at the inn? We may never know—but we do know that Mary and Joseph were led by God regardless of the irritation of the situation. When they were confronted with the reality of no room at the inn, Joseph didn't say, "Hey, Mary, let's go a little further to Herodium or maybe go a little back to Bethany. Let's see if they have rooms available there instead…hold on, baby, I got this!" No, Joseph and Mary stayed where they were, and somehow they ended up in a place where animals slept—and Jesus was born right where God said He would be. All the drama didn't matter then. God's will was done and angels filled the sky to celebrate the birth.

God's Word is *going* to come to pass, whether the devil fights it or not and whether people understand it or not. If God says, "My Son is coming and this is where He will be," then that's where He will be—and that holds true whether it's being born in a certain town or coming back through a certain gate! God's will is going to be done. If God said it, don't just accept it. *Believe* it and look forward to it because, buddy, that is what is *going* to happen! I don't care if God said it five thousand years ago or yesterday, it's coming to pass.

Chapter 2

God's Work Doesn't Appeal to Our Senses: It's Not Always Comfortable, But It Is Always Best

Sometimes we want to look to our natural senses and use them as evidence for spiritual things—and if Mary and Joseph had done that, they probably would have thought that God had abandoned them. They had a new baby on the way, were about to be hit with possible greater taxes, and there wasn't even a place for them at the inn once they got to Bethlehem. By all outward accounts, they might have wondered if God's plan was coming to pass at all.

Things happen in the spirit that we can't always properly gauge with our natural senses. Faith itself requires us to "call those things that be not as if they already were"—to act as if our prayers have already been answered, to embody the spiritual solution instead of the natural problem, and to set our eyes on things above—even as we walk here below Heaven, on earth.

Faith is trusting God's plan more than our natural senses. Faith is speaking the end result instead of the current situation. Faith is meditating on the Word until the principle of that verse becomes "bigger" in our own minds than the natural circumstances around us.

What can we imagine? What dreams do we have deep in our hearts? What has God said to us, shown to us, and how has He told us to stretch ourselves for His best? We like to think that God's best is always going to be marked by comfort—but that is not often the case.

GOD'S BEST ISN'T ALWAYS COMFORTABLE

Faith is uncomfortable. Being led by our senses is comfortable. Thinking naturally whatever thoughts we want, complaining, commiserating with others, and "telling it like it is" is comfortable. Why? Because we have done it so much! It's habit. We are made of both the dust of the earth and the breath of God. If we only live like dust, we will only experience the shallow breath of God in our own heart—but if we sow to the spirit, we are taking deeper and deeper breaths from God's Spirit within us. This is not comfortable! But it is better.

Don't be a shallow breather—you were created to think higher, speak higher, and live higher than your natural senses. As believers who understand the value of the Spirit of God within us and the truth of His Word, we should aim to never live by emotional whims of our flesh. It may make us feel good temporarily, but we will miss out on a deeper walk with God and more powerful and fulfilled life if we brave the discomfort of living by faith.

We must realize that God's Word—His truth and the principles for a good life—as well as the work He does, often doesn't always appeal to the natural man's senses. If we only did what our senses told us to do all the time, we'd end up flitting from one thing to the other without much direction.

The Word gives us direction and guidance. Faith in that Word helps us to choose God's truth over our own senses. So, when things happen that seem to blow us off course, we can remind ourselves that we aren't moved by what we see, but we are moved by what we believe.

Just like Jesus needed to be in the right place at the right time, so we need to be in the right place at the right time—and we get there by trusting the Holy Spirit is guiding the situations in our life and will prompt us to do what we need to do at the exact moment needed to move us where we need to be.

We must remind ourselves that God is bigger than any circumstance and that most of the discomfort we may feel is just us giving up our own ideas about "how God should do this or that." We cannot judge God's way of doing things and expect to feel good— we feel better when we let go of our own ideas about exactly how He should or should not do something and simply trust that His plan is the best plan—and that the Holy Spirit within us will prompt us and show us when we are being hindered by Satan or simply being moved by the hand of God.

WE RELEASE OUR WILL IN FAVOR OF GOD'S WILL

As believers, we release our will in favor of God's will because we know that He is with us, He will never leave us or forsake us, and in the end we *win*. Just like that old cliché that "You can't have a testimony unless you have a test," we remember that God's ways aren't man's ways, and a lot of times the thing we think is a "test" is just us resisting God's unusual plan!

We aren't called to resist God—we are called to resist the devil. The Word tells us to submit ourselves to God and to resist the devil (which also means anything against God's love/light/goodness). If we do both, then the devil will flee from us. God won't make the devil flee; *we* make him flee.

You cannot just attend church once a week or just watch church on the internet and think you are becoming a more spiritually-minded person. Faith in God is a lifestyle, and it starts with God and you together. It is a shifting of your will toward His, knowing that His will is in your best interests and in the best interests of others in the world. We are connected.

If we look at our society and don't like what we see, it is only because our society is made up of our people and our people are not living well—and living well starts in the mind, and whatever we allow to remain there will seep into our hearts. Misguided, foolish, and dark thoughts breed lives that are lived the exact same way. We reap what we sow, in every single way. "The blind leading the blind" is such a good way to explain it, because that is exactly what it is oftentimes. People fall into the ditches of life all the time, but they start falling in their mind and heart before they ever see it in their actual lives.

Darkness is simply an absence of light. So, in the absence of God's light and goodness, people often begin to downgrade their thoughts, words, and actions. We want to *upgrade* our thoughts, our words, and our actions—and there is no better upgrade than to align ourselves with God's Word.

It's easy to see when a person has hit rock bottom in *life*. It's hard to sometimes see when a person has hit rock bottom in their heart. Plenty of successful looking people are at the bottom when it comes to the way they think, talk, and live. Think about it. How many chase money just to find that they still aren't happy, even if they can buy whatever they want? How many chase exciting love just to find they still aren't fulfilled by a rotating cast of sexual partners? How many chase only the pleasures of life just to later find out that still, in the deep of the night, they do not feel fulfilled in their hearts?

TEMPORARY PLEASURES CAN'T FULFILL SPIRITUAL NEEDS

Emotional feelings are normal and good, but they change all the time so you can't really trust them. We shouldn't put our trust in anything/anyone that is marked by such instability. This is why our senses are not good guides for our best lives—no matter how many people repeat that you should just follow your bliss or joy, or whatever, it's not true. Follow God's best for your life, and you will have much more lasting joy, along with a great many moments of bliss.

God is stable and secure—our spirit within us is powerful, and the more we tap into it and live by it, the better we think, talk, and live. As believers, we have a lot of fun, a lot of adventure, and a lot of curveballs thrown at us in life too—but we aren't derailed off of our faith by any of it. God is our constant. The Holy Spirit is our guide. Like Mary and Joseph, we just move when we must, stop when we must, and rest in the peace that God is with us in *everything*.

If we let go of what we think "should" happen and aim for our goals (what He's told us or put in our heart to do) with both laser focus and adaptability, we are going to have a much more peaceful journey in life—regardless of what we "see." Like Mary and Joseph, we just probably won't care if we end up in a fancy hotel, a little inn, or a manger in a field…as long as Jesus is there, we are going to be more than OK!

SUCCESS AS A BELIEVER ISN'T A ONE-SIDED VENTURE

If you have God in your heart and His Word in your mouth, *you* are not lacking. If you don't like the way your life is now, remind yourself of this, "My God has everything I need and His principles will get me where I need and desire to be—I'm going somewhere good in my thoughts today, because my focus is on *Him* and His plan for my life. I don't need to be fixed because I'm not broken—Jesus fixed my spiritual condition at the cross, and now all I need is practice His Word. I am a new creature in Christ and old things are passed away, everything is becoming new. New thoughts. New words. New actions. I align myself with God's Word and move His way. I'm not going where I've already been—faith in God and faith in myself are taking me someplace new. If it's uncomfortable, I don't care. I am up for the ride, I'm down for the journey, and will move mountains with my faith!"

Success as a believer isn't a one-sided venture. It's the ability to get where you have pointed yourself—the direction God is calling you, and the direction of the dreams and desires He has placed within. You can and will adapt easily when you put your trust in God. Fear takes you out of ease. Faith puts your heart at ease. That's how you know if you're in fear or faith. There is no "worry" in faith. There may be concern. There may be curiosity. But worry is just a cousin of fear—and it might come over now and again, but it's not meant to stay! You kick it out of your mind by shifting to faith and trusting God for the journey of your day. You point yourself in the right direction, and that is where you'll go—even if it looks like a detour, you are working on something!

Success is living God's way and experiencing abundance in *all* areas of life. It's not religion (manmade rules and ideas) that sets people free for abundance. It's Christ's sacrifice on the cross that changes the spiritual direction of your life, and it's God's revolutionary Word that changes the thought process of your mind. When your spirit and your mind are one—not pulling against each other—your faith changes things quicker.

Most of the battles we have are in our own mind. When we get our mind right and line ourselves up with what He said instead of what we see, we start talking different and it's a course *far* above our natural senses. I notice that people with a lack mentality tend to always say what they *have*—but people with an abundance mentality tend to do the opposite and say what they *want*.

Faith sees what others don't see. It's like you grow eyes in your spirit, and you relax even when you have a big goal. You "see" it in the Word or it bubbles up in your spirit and you go for it in your mind first. You aren't a wisher; you become a dreamer who acts on his or her dreams. You don't want one thing but go out and do the opposite. No, you align yourself with what God said—and you point yourself in that direction. You aim to not only get where God said you could go, but to get there the right way. Success isn't just the right numbers in your bank account or whatever dream you may have coming to pass—success is also getting there without losing your mind! You can aim for big things, you can see God's plan come to pass, and you don't have to wring your hands in pure misery to get there.

REFUSE TO BE "STRESSED OUT"— CHOOSE FAITH IN GOD AND YOURSELF INSTEAD

Rich but miserable and in constant stress isn't success to me. Perfect on the outside but tormented on the inside isn't success to me. I love God and all His principles and ways, and I notice that the more I put into it, the more success comes out of Him and into me—an abundant type of success that affects every area of my life for the better. I literally absorb *His* mentality when I meditate on His Word, and let me tell you something—that is one abundant mentality! There's no "stressed out" when the Holy Spirit is guiding you. None.

The world would have you living from one anxious thought to another. They are in the business of making miserable people! They are in the business of feeding your fears. Many products and businesses run on the fears of people—they aren't out for your best interests but are out to make money off of your feelings of lack!

God didn't call us to misery; He called us to joy, because joy is a fruit of His Spirit. You can have peace even if you have a lot to do. Being busy doesn't have to equal being stressed out. Take a look at what you're doing to make sure you actually need to be doing it. The world will lead you to believe that "being busy" equals success in a way. But sometimes we put too much stress on ourselves for no good reason other than to feel like we are "doing something"—and if that's the case, it's often because we are ignoring our spirit. People will load themselves up with all sorts of things just to deny their own spirit nagging at them, even Christians!

Jesus said it best when He told us not to worry about tomorrow because today has enough trouble of its own! In other words, don't fill up your mind with useless worries—deal with today, and deal with it as it comes up. Trust the God who trusts in you. Realize that how you are doing anything is just as important as what you are actually doing.

The older I get the more I realize that enjoying what you are doing, in the moment you are doing it, is more important than racing to the next thing. I am accomplishing more today than I did when I was young, and I'm enjoying reaching my goals even more. I don't believe it's good to run around like a chicken with your head cut off racing through your own life. Life is a vapor and you don't want to make it go any faster just by living with a racing brain.

"Stressed out" is a mindset that comes out of fear—fear you "can't do it all" or fear things "won't go according to my plan" or fear that "if I don't do it nobody else will!" etc. Fear says, "I can't," but faith says, "I can do all things through Christ who gives me strength!" The mindset shift is invaluable, because you can't slow down or speed up the time—but you can change how you perceive what is going on at any given moment. The Word is our backbone for changing stressful thoughts (fear) into peaceful thoughts (faith). But you will never be able to make the shift daily if you don't sow the Word into your own mind. You have to have something to pull from. Make time for the Word, and the Word will help you to make time for you.

REALIZE THAT YOU ARE DEPLETABLE: THERE'S A REASON WHY FAITH COMES BY "HEARING AND HEARING"

Often, we just don't realize that we are depletable. We think the Word we heard last Sunday is enough. No, unless you are going to sleep from this Sunday to next Sunday, you need to meditate on the principles of God's Word daily—because you live daily. The reason faith comes by hearing and hearing (repetition) of the Word of God is because we are human, and we are depletable. Just like we drive our car and need to fill up with gas, we live our lives and need to fill up with faith.

So, if you hit a slump and feel yourself chugging out, guess what? You let yourself go too long without filling up. Don't beat yourself up about it, just get to the gas station—stop, pray, be still, and know that He is God. Recognize that you aren't God! You need God. He's not going to come and ding you on the forehead with a wand and make all your thoughts better for you—He's given you His Word and His Spirit, and His grace is sufficient for you. Fill up with it.

After you pray and are still, start speaking the Word over yourself. Move your thoughts to His thoughts, His ways, knowing they are higher than your human thoughts and ways. As you meditate on His Word and speak it, you start getting the "mind of Christ," which means an anointed mind—a mind that is not bogged down with just natural things. It will shift your emotions. I can't tell you how many times I end up shouting in my car because the Spirit of God has come all over me!

Those times you have with God are important—they help to remind you that you aren't walking through your life alone. You've got Heaven backing you! So, if the plan doesn't seem like it's going right to you, remember that Jesus came on the scene in a circumstance that didn't seem "right" either!

THE ROAD MAY BE WINDING, BUT IT ENDS WHERE IT SHOULD

Yet Jesus was exactly where He needed to be. The manger was a metaphor. Think about it. Christ who lived in Heaven was comfortable walking on gold streets or sleeping in the hay! His circumstance did not dictate Who He was or what He did or where He was going!

As a man, Jesus' "comfort" was in the Father's plan more than any earthly comfort or discomfort. Jesus chose the Father's will over anything else. Why? Because He had something to do. He needed to save us! He knew that God had a plan, and He did not want to divert from that good plan.

To be comfortable whether you abase or abound is a Christian mindset—it is a contented mindset that says, "No matter where I am, I am at rest in my soul. Even if I'm busy, I am at rest inside. Jesus did not stay in the manger. He did not live in hay. Today He is seated at the right hand of the Father in Heaven, the highest of places. So, regardless of where I started, I'll finish well too! Regardless of where I am, there is a higher place to go…and I'm going! God's plan for my life is good." Never deceive yourself about small beginnings. Jesus began in a manger and is on the throne today. All of us are born to rise!

Lean on the good plan of God and you will see that when you stick with Him, and when you apply His principles with the right heart, you are going nowhere else but *up*. The road may be winding, but it ends where it should. Heaven is your final destination, and you will be talking about your time here on earth there too.

Give your future eternal self something to celebrate! Live your life now in line with God's best—start now to have a "heavenly mindset" and choose to think from a place of abundance instead of lack. Realize that no matter where you are now, abundance begins with a full heart of faith. So, sow the Word into your heart knowing that only the Word will last forever.

The Holy Spirit can lift you up or calm you down, whatever you need in the moment for the position you are currently at in life. Realize that your "gas tank" can get low and you are depletable inside—but God's Word and the Holy Spirit within you can fill you back up again! You have everything you need in God's Word to meet every goal or desire He's placed on your heart. No matter what His plan or what good goal/desire you have in mind, you can do it with peace and you can do it with grace, but only if you do it with God.

ABUNDANCE IS A DIVINE MINDSET

My ministry is marked by abundance. Although I preach on all kinds of different topics in the Word and rarely speak just on finances or abundant living, it seems like everywhere I go someone is either 1) asking me about *how* to live a more abundant life or 2) telling me I'm *wrong* for believing that it's godly to live an abundant life.

My life speaks for itself, and I guess it speaks loudly! I don't just teach abundant living; I believe it and live it—without excuses. I never make an excuse for the blessings of God on my life. I don't hide my blessings in fear of what others may say or think. They are going to talk anyway, no matter what I do. I'm firm in my belief that God is good and if Jesus came to give me life and life more abundantly (and that is what He said He came for in John 10:10), then I don't see any reason I should have to cower to people who don't believe what Jesus said.

I serve Christ, not Christians. I feel zero shame or guilt for believing in the works and teachings of Jesus—and I believe that whatever area I choose to focus my faith upon will expand my mind, ignite my heart, and change my life. That's what God's Word has done for me and it's a daily practice for me to stretch myself in my own faith in the Word of God.

When I was younger, I thought I could only believe God for one area at a time. I was limited in my thinking so I limited myself. I hadn't grown enough in my own faith in God to realize how *big* He really is—or how the principle of abundance begins in the mind.

Abundance is a divine mindset. When we allow ourselves to accept it and put faith in God's power, well, we can change all sorts of things in our own life. We take off the limits. Then, we continue to do that—even when everything around us in the natural seems to say, "you can't do that." I always say, "Watch me!"

GOD'S BEST IS THE "BEST CHOICE" FOR YOU

God is a Spirit and we who worship Him do it in spirit and in truth. This means that godly abundance is a spiritual concept first. We may see the earthly effects but it began with God, the One Who is more than enough. *More* is a great word. More is what God is— He's way more than we can imagine.

Many people live in a state of mind that can only be described as a "lack mentality." They may have come by that mindset honestly through childhood or the experiences of their own lives, and some may even defend lack as holy—lack is a sacred cow. I believe that if lack itself is holy, then Heaven must be the most unholy place there is! It's not. So, I don't care if a person says lack is good because it's just not true.

Your parents may have brought you up with a lack mindset—you can change it once you acknowledge that what God says is truer than your upbringing. If society at large has continually fed you a mental diet of "you can't/you'll never" and "somebody will succeed but not you," well, you can change that too—but first you have to acknowledge that the mindset itself exists, and it's just a lie somebody told you. "You" aren't what you've been told, if what you have been told goes against God's Word. You are God's child and created for abundance—that's your identity. It's not your job or your talent or anything else.

Abundance isn't just a nice home, a good college or trade school for your kid, a new car or a dream vacation—although of course it can include all that if you want. Abundance is a lifestyle of choosing God's best no matter what it is. God's best is love, and not hatred. His best is peace, and not strife. God's best is health, and not sickness. God's best is abundance, and not poverty. God's best is joy, and not misery. You get the idea. All of it is the abundant choice.

Think of God's best as the "best choice" for you, at any given moment—and not just for you, but for your family, church, community, and for the whole world. If there were no fear of scarcity or loss, giving would be easier for a lot of people. I've often said that people share more when they are full...not when they are hungry!

So, when you get a "full" mindset, you are much more prone to give of yourself in various ways. You get excited when you see someone else get blessed because you know that their blessings don't take anything away from you—so you don't fear others' success; you just are happy for them, as you should be. God has enough for us all! There is no lack in God. Let that sink in until it becomes your automatic thought.

EVEN YOUR THOUGHTS ARE "SEEDS"—SOW ABUNDANTLY

As God's children, we are linked together too, like it or not! What one person does affects the other. What groups do affect even more people. Even if nobody around you supports the idea that you are created to live abundantly, choose abundance. It's God's way! I believe that God made man to do something in life—even before the fall, Adam had a job of tending the garden. He was supposed to be fruitful, multiply, replenish, and subdue. Those were the four main requirements for both his life and his work. So, God put sowing and reaping, replenishing and subduing right there at the beginning for a reason—because this is what we need to do in life.

God's chosen system of giving/receiving or sowing/reaping is our best choice for getting to a state of abundance in all areas of life. What we sow, we will reap. If we sow to the spirit, we receive something different than if we sow to the flesh. If we continually sow anger into our own minds, what do you think will show up in our lives? More things to be angry about! If we continually sow kindness and mercy toward ourselves even, what do you think we will experience the most in our everyday life? Kindness and mercy will come back to us. So, the angry get more angry and more reasons to be angry just like the loving get more loving and more reasons to show more love.

We get what we are looking for because the very focus of our mind is a mental seed that we are sowing—and we reap what we sow. So, if your mind consistently focuses on the disappointments of life, the curveballs, and struggles—well, what do you think you're sowing toward? More of the same.

If you don't want to repeat the same struggles, then it's time to change the seeds you're sowing in your head—and renewing your mind to think more abundantly is a great place to start!

The Word has the power to transform your entire life, to break old patterns, and to begin new ways of living—but it only will transform your life to the degree that you think it, speak it, and do it.

OTHER PEOPLE IN GOD'S PLAN FOR **YOUR** LIFE

A lot of times, we don't understand why something is taking so long to get done—but we must understand that God uses people to push His plan for our lives along, and how we respond to the events in our life can make all the difference in the world. We can stay "stuck" complaining or we can not "get weary in well doing" knowing that if we stick with God, we are on the right path regardless of the time.

In Luke chapter 6, verse 38, it refers to financial giving when it says, "Give and it shall be given unto you." It tells you that what you get in return will be a "good measure, pressed down, shaken together, and running over" amount of return. But I want you to notice that it doesn't fall from the sky. How do you reap? It says, "men give unto your bosom." So, the world works by giving and receiving—and people are the ones doing both.

Now, you aren't supposed to walk around asking, "Are you the man who's supposed to give to me?" If you do that, you miss the spiritual concept looking for the physical man. God is our Source, but He uses people. Those who give are given more. Those who take have even what they have taken away. The reason is because sowing and reaping works both ways. Nothing is stagnant in the world.

When your mindset is abundance, you don't scan the horizon all day begging anybody who is in your path to give to you. You give and you expect to reap, because you know that's the principle God put in place—so you have faith in it, and faith means calling those things that be not as though they were (Romans 4:17). So, you begin speaking it. "I am a giver and I am blessed. I have more than enough, my cup runs over! Finances come to me all the time. I am a good steward of what I have, and I give more as more comes in. Every day I'm increasing. God causes others to give to me, and I give to overs, I keep the cycle of blessing going in my life. Finances come in increasing amounts, from unexpected sources, on a continual basis. Everything I do God's way prospers. I have all I need and desire— spiritually, physically, and financially! I'm blessed!"

You aren't saying those kinds of things to people in order to get them to do something for you—you are speaking them into your own heart and putting God in remembrance of His Word too. You are reinforcing a truth by speaking it out. So, you are sowing God's Word and His Word will not come back to Him void. It will fulfill itself! People will bless you. You will have favor, opportunities, unexpected blessings—and as they come, your job is to be grateful and praise God, and give again, keeping the cycle of blessing going.

GOD HAS NOT CALLED
THE CHURCH TO BE A LEECH

As a minister, I meet a lot of people. I meet a lot of successful people too—I don't try and get close to them just because I know they have money to help the cause of Christ, even though I know the cause of Christ is worth giving toward. No! *God* moves upon people, and that means it's not my job to try to move people!

For example, I am not going to pretend to like golf just because some guy with a lot of money plays golf in an effort to get him to "give unto my bosom!" I would *not* like it if somebody did that to me, so I'm not doing that to anybody else. I think when preachers do that, it's abusive and I consider it like prostituting the anointing of God. I refuse to do it. I trust that God can do His job, and He will bless this ministry with everything it needs to fulfill the vision He gave us.

So, God uses people to bless you in the city, in the field, coming in, and going out—and He will use them whether they are saved or not—but our eyes should be focused on God and His principles. God has not called the Church to be a leech. God moves upon people to support the work, no matter whether they're saved or unsaved.

So, when I pray for God to bless me, I say, "Lord, You cause men to give unto my bosom. I don't even need to know who the men are. It don't make a lick of difference whether they're saved or unsaved, but I'm going to get Your job done." I expect it to happen so I don't live with fear that it won't—that is my faith working with me to bring about manifestation. Do you understand what I am saying? I know that God will bring favor where there is no favor. He'll bring love where there is no love. He will bring lightness where there is only heaviness—He will open doors that no man can shut, and move upon men and women to get behind good works.

A person with a lack mindset will say things like, "This ain't going to work. I don't see how it's going to happen. I don't know anybody with that much money. This vision costs too much." A person with an abundant mindset knows that he/she doesn't have to know *how* it's going to happen; they just know it's going to happen! Like Jesus born in Bethlehem, it's going to happen. Period. End of statement!

When I'm out eating (which I do a lot of because Cathy isn't into cooking!) I always meet people who say things like, "You know, I'm not into this God stuff, but I watch you all the time." I find it amazing how many people who openly say they don't believe in God watch me on TV or the web. Many of them will literally put money in my hand "for the ministry" right after they tell me they aren't into God! Why? What's happening? The unconscious obedience of unbelievers—that's what's happening. God causing men to give unto my bosom—that's what's happening.

I've had unbelievers tell me, "You know, sometimes I watch you and you make me feel like doing things I wouldn't normally do." They don't even know why they suddenly want to give, or be more kind, or help others. They are being moved upon by God and don't even see it. Yet! I consider my ministry a seed-planting work—and even if I don't harvest the soul, so to speak, the seed has been planted and I have faith that it will spring up. I'm not sowing my personality; I'm sowing the Word of God through my personality and there is a difference. The anointing of God is on His Word.

Chapter 3

No Work of God Is Devoid of Power, His Promises Will Always Come to Pass

I've seen my wife, Cathy, heavy with child—I mean, she looked like she was pushing a pointed barge! She was only 95 pounds when she got pregnant and at the top weight of her pregnancy she was 115 pounds. But when we went to the hospital so that she could have our baby, her belly was so big she looked like every pound she had was right there in the middle!

Even though I was about to be a first-time father, I didn't worry when they wheeled her into the room. I knew without a shadow of a doubt that Cathy was in good hands with that doctor and with that nurse. I knew that those medical professionals knew their job—they knew what they were doing and I trusted my wife to their care.

I didn't assess the situation and say, "Hey, doc, I think you're doing it wrong right there, gimme those forceps!" Why? Because I *knew* that I didn't know anything about delivering a baby! I didn't overstep my position. You see, I knew how to create a baby, but I didn't know what to do in order to birth a baby. So I let that doctor do the job I was paying him to do.

When it comes to applying the Word, it's your job to create things with the words of your mouth and the meditations of your heart—but it's God's job to birth those things. He is the deliverer! Let God do His job.

God is not called the Almighty for nothing. Everything He does is marked by His own power—and no work of God is devoid of power. When God uses someone you never thought He would use, it's a testament to His ability and will to move that particular person. He didn't pick them out of a hat. He chose them to help facilitate His plan, and His purpose is His own. Remember that no work of God is devoid of power—His work will always affirm His almightiness and faithfulness.

GOD'S POWER AFFIRMS HIS ALMIGHTINESS AND FAITHFULNESS

If you are believing God for your healing, what is your job? How do you create the atmosphere for healing? You begin by saying what the Word says, "By His stripes I am healed." You may think, *But I feel pain.* This is not the time to say what you *have*; it's the time to say what you *want*—you aren't denying the present, you are creating the future with the words of God. You are dealing with something serious, your health, so it's time to be serious about the Word. You decide that you are going to do your job and be diligent—because your body depends on it. You change the circumstances with the words of your mouth, the meditations of your heart, and the actions you take that align with what you are creating. Every time your mind wants to tell you something different, you bring those thoughts into captivity—to the obedience of God's Word. You call those things which be not until they are.

Whatever it is that you want to create in your own life, you will need to begin with the thoughts in your own head. And if you want what God says, then you need to say what God says. That's your job. He does His. And together, your life grows, heals, expands, and gets better and better. It's abundance of whatever it is that you are wanting. Abundance of health, prosperity, peace, joy—whatever it is that you desire.

God will move people into place, and some will recognize God is using them while others may not. Your job is just to align yourself with God's Word—not just in word, but in thought and action—and watch Him bring it to pass. All the promises of God are yea and amen, according to 2 Corinthians 1:20, which means yes and so be it! So, say "yes" and "so be it" to the Word that has the power to quicken your mortal body and bring the desires of your heart to pass. Don't fight what you really want by doubting your Father, the Creator of everything that exists. No work of God is devoid of power, and it's His power that affirms His almightiness and faithfulness.

WE MUST LOOK FORWARD TO THE FUTURE WITH FIRM CONVICTION

At Christmas, it's natural to feel nostalgic—we tend to look back, and sometimes that is with joy and other times it is with sorrow. We often have this idea in our head that is formed by movies and other things that Christmas should be a certain way, and that people should act a certain way—and some may be tempted to focus so much on the actual gifts that they lose sight of the kindness itself in giving. It's a blessing to be given anything at all. It's a blessing that someone thought of you.

If you allow what you get or how people act to dictate whether you will be happy celebrating Christmas day or not, you are giving them too much power. It's not other people's job to make you happy and fulfilled. Joy is from the Lord and it's in your spirit. You can tap into it at any moment—but you have to take the pressure off of yourself and others. You don't have to "make Christmas perfect." It's not a holiday to perform as if your family is on the big screen. It's a holiday to be authentic in your love, joy, and generosity as a celebration of Jesus Christ. That's what makes it the most wonderful time of the year.

Jesus came! God sent His only Son. That is the greatest gift we could ever get. Anything else anyone gives or does for you, if the food happens to be good or everybody happens to get along, well, that's just a bonus! If you fix your eyes on people to meet all your desires, you just may have a very disappointing holiday season.

The love Christ has for you is personal and deep, and it blows away any gift anybody can wrap. Draw close, fix your eyes on Him, and remind yourself that everything you are doing is really about honoring Him. So, when you give, give with a pure heart. When you receive, receive with gratitude. Choose to be blessed by whatever comes your way. It's not about how much money you spend on a gift or how many gifts you get. It's a few weeks out of the year when people all over the world unite under a spirit of giving and love— and the reason is because of the Christ child, no matter what the shops say!

JESUS—HE DIDN'T STAY
IN THE MANGER

I'm thrilled God came in human form, but focusing on Jesus as a baby isn't really the best way to think about God in the flesh. Jesus is not a baby anymore. He outgrew that stage quickly and there is a reason why there isn't much in the Word about His time as a baby—and it's because it doesn't hold a candle to the teachings He gave us in adulthood, His sacrifice on the cross for our redemption, and the promise of His return.

If you think Jesus surprised the world when He was born, just wait until He returns! It's going to shock the socks off people—and just like His birth changed everything, His return will change everything. The next part of God's plan is Jesus' *return* and that may be sooner than you think. God will move people into place. He will influence both believers and unbelievers. God will make sure that His plan comes to pass.

Traditional Christmas celebrations will always shift your focus *back*. But I encourage you to see the *future* in that manger. Your future. The future of the world. The plan of God is still in action. The whole plan was housed in that little baby—but the baby is all grown up! Jesus is in Heaven waiting for the Father to say, "Go get them!"

The King of Kings, the Rose of Sharon, the Lily of the Valley, and the Bright and Morning Star! Through Mary, He became a biological member of the human race. I've often asked myself: "Why?" God could have done things another way, but He chose to put on flesh and be with us.

JESUS—THE GOD WHO COULD BE TOUCHED

You couldn't hug God before Jesus came. Yet, when God took on a fleshly form in the person of Jesus, children could not only come close, but also sit on His lap. Can you imagine being held by the God of all Creation? It was our human flesh that gave God the ability to dampen down His glory enough for us to stand it and not just blow up under the intensity of His glory. There is a reason we are going to need incorruptible bodies. Maybe God became human because He wanted us to be able to see Him, touch Him, and hear His voice too.

I don't know why, but every time I think of that, I am reminded of my daddy and a one-toed bird he named George. My daddy bought this parrot, and he loved him. I don't know why he loved him because George was as mean as a snake. The only reason we had the bird was because nobody else wanted him. George had lost two toes and only had one to hold on to the perch—but Daddy fell in love when he saw that bird and had to have him, and so George lived in the kitchen.

Daddy wanted that bird to talk so bad, so he'd say, "George boooy, the dear boooy" over and over and over. So this crazy bird began to say, "George boooy, the dear boooy." And once he said that, he started saying everything. You had to watch what you said around George. If you cussed, George would cuss too. He was really smart, but he was still mean. If you put your finger in his cage and you weren't my daddy, he would flat cut your finger with his beak! You better not put it in far; you just might lose the whole thing. George was rough. Now, he'd let Daddy touch him, but not much. Oh, but Daddy wanted to hold that bird. He was always talking about it and leaning in like he might take him out of the cage and try.

"Don't do that, Daddy," I'd say, "George will kill you. You think he likes you. Look at him! He's looking at you like this!" and I'd make a face. "He don't like ya, Daddy! You're always making fun of his toe and he heard that!" Daddy didn't listen to me. He'd just look at George with love and laugh and talk about his toe. George hated us all, but out of all of us, he hated Daddy a little bit less.

So one time, Daddy took a paper bag, shoved it over George so he couldn't see, and pulled him up to his face and just hugged him—fast! George couldn't see anything and Daddy was so happy hugging that bird in a bag. I waited looking at that thinking, *If that bag slips, if Daddy decides to lift it a little and George sees what's going on, Daddy is gonna lose his nose! That bird is going to take it clean off!*

I guess George liked Daddy more than I thought, because Daddy did lift that bag up and George just wanted to get back in his cage—took his one toe and twirled around and made it back to where he wanted to be. George could do amazing things with just one toe. He fascinated me, even though I hated his stinking guts because he always told on me when I tried to sneak food out of the fridge at night. "Jesse's in the fridge! Jesse's in the fridge!" he'd holler and I'd get so mad, I'd want to knock him off his perch. He only had that one toe, so I thought I could do it, but George wasn't having it—he'd snap so fast, I'd pull my finger out before he could get me and just cuss.

You couldn't do anything around that bird because he was so smart. He didn't just repeat stuff, he could think! And if he didn't know what to say, he'd just go to squawking so loud that somebody would show up to tell you to quit whatever you were doing.

Well, sometimes I laugh and think that, just like Daddy wanted to hug George, God wanted to hug us—even if we are a nasty, surly, and sometimes mean bunch of people. God still loves us. Even when we're snapping at Him, He still loves us. Maybe we've been beat up and are hobbling around like a one-toed parrot—I think God sees it all, and has mercy on us because He doesn't just know the details of what happened in our lives, He knows the intentions of our heart.

Maybe God came down as Jesus because He just wanted to be close to us—to walk with us and hug on us, and show us how to live better and more loving lives. God knows we won't be here long. He knows it's just a vapor. His perspective is so different from ours because it's eternal. But I believe He enjoyed being with Adam, walking in the cool of the day, before Adam was corrupted by sin and lost whatever made him able to be in God's presence without burning up.

God came to be with us. It's the reason we have Christmas. And He's going to enjoy being with us in Heaven, too. We serve a loving God, a good Father, Who still has plans in the works. We may not know all of His plans, but we do know that Jesus is coming back—which means God is coming back. We can trust Him to follow through with what He said and we can trust that He is with us every step of the way on our own life journey too—all we've got to do is stay close to Him and we can be sure that He will stay close to us.

No Christmas party on this earth and no gift given or received can possibly compare with what awaits us—whether we cross over through earthly death or He comes back while we are still living here—whichever comes first, the end result will be the same. We will once again be face to face with God.

Don't Worry or Get in a Hurry—Due Season Is Coming

If God could use a man like Caesar Augustus, and God could use a man like Cyrus too, can He use men in power today? Has He used political figures in the past? You better know it! Even if they were unconscious of it, some were used by God—because when God has a plan, He makes sure to bring it to fruition.

So, if you are worried about anything in your life, if there are things you are believing for, let your mind be at ease in Christ—remember that Christ the hope of glory lives in you. You have a Comforter in the Holy Spirit. He can lift your emotions and give you peace even in circumstances that leave you feeling low. Your worry melts in the light of His presence because love itself is a purging and cleansing thing—it can cast out all fear, and He will if you let Him in. We submit to the Lord and trust Him, and it brings peace. If we choose not to do that, then we can get comfortable in our own misery.

The Bible says, *"Howbeit when He, the Spirit of truth, is come, He will guide you into all truth"* (John 16:13). Has He come? Yes. Will He guide you in all truth? Yes. If you submit yourself to Him and allow your faith in Him to rise, you will access His guidance—worrying, begging, and pleading doesn't help. Faith helps. So, choose faith. Choose to trust.

Give God your all, and not just a little bit of your faith. Fill up when you need more because you've used it up. Keep moving forward knowing that everything God said, He will do. You don't have to worry or get in a hurry. God's plans for you will come to pass. Be not weary in well doing because you will reap if you faint *not*.

Whatever you are sowing is coming back. Don't quit "well doing" just because you don't see your manifestation yet. Don't be like those people who stopped caring about babies born in Bethlehem because the prophecy seemed to have passed. In due season, we reap. In due season, our faith manifests results. In due season, God orchestrates His plan down to the last tiny bit. Nothing He does is devoid of power, and soon enough you will see yourself propelled by that power and His promise to you will come to pass.

Chapter 4

Caesar Wanted to Meet the Needs of a Government, Jesus Came to Meet the Needs of the People

Caesar was thinking about himself when he decided that he wanted more taxes from the people. His goal was to meet the needs of a government, but Jesus was on His way to meet the needs of the people.

How can God meet all your needs according to His riches in glory? Do you think this verse is only about the day-to-day physical needs of life? The greater depth of that familiar verse has to do with Jesus Christ, I believe—because the greatest need mankind has is in the heart. All of the issues of life flow out the heart, which is why we're warned to keep our heart right and do it with all the diligence we can muster.

It seems odd that God would use unbelievers, but God can do anything and He often does things we just wouldn't think He would do. It's also odd that He tells believers to set aside their own conscience at times in order to be accepting of what unbelievers offer us. If a heathen offers a devout Jew food that has been literally offered to idols, which are often demons posing as demi-gods, God says to eat it anyway—just because the unbeliever gave it to you. Now, it seems like a no-brainer to reject something like that if you love God, and yet God says to do it. Again, God is mysterious and has His reasons for even the odd things He says.

This reminds me of a time once, years ago, when I had a high-ranking official in my state government request to meet me. I wasn't involved in anything political and didn't even know all the officials' names in my state government. I knew the governor, etc., but I wasn't familiar with this particular man. I decided to meet him anyway at a service I was scheduled to be preaching at in a small church. This church was filled with blue-collar workers and lower income people. I go to all sorts of churches—big, small, and everywhere in between. As long as I feel led by the Lord to be there, I book the meeting and I don't worry about whether a church can meet my ministry's needs or not—I truly believe in living by faith. God will provide for the ministry He's established. It's not my job to do God's job!

Well, the man walked into the church and I noticed that he had a small paper sack in his hand. It was about the size of the paper bags they give you when you buy candy or a quart of milk. He was cordial, but not chatty. He asked me how I was doing and I said I was just fine, and he handed the bag to me. "We'd like to bless you," he said. I looked in the bag and it was a stack of cash. It was ten thousand dollars. Now, I'm accustomed to some people giving large donations—but this is always done by check! And everybody wants a tax-deductible receipt for their giving when the amount is so big.

"Oh, sir!" I said, "Thank you. What is your name again? I will give you a receipt for the donation." He flat refused. He didn't want a receipt. Now, it's not every day that a man gives a paper sack of money to the ministry—that is a very unusual thing. I didn't think he was a believer. He said nothing about God, although he did use the word "bless," but he seemed extremely uncomfortable. He left pretty quickly with a look on his face like he'd done what he came to do, and now it was time for him to just get out of the church.

What that man didn't realize, and I didn't say, was that ten thousand dollars was the exact amount I had been believing God for in prayer to come in for the ministry. I let my own conscience go about it, knowing that while I had no idea where that money came from, it couldn't have been on the "up-and-up" if it came in a paper bag! I considered that a "Caesar Augustus" kind of thing—where the unconscious obedience of an unbeliever ends up making things happen for you. God uses them, and they don't even realize it.

I sometimes wonder if God moves upon unbelievers as a last resort after believers have said no to something He's asked them to do. Believers don't always believe or obey—but sometimes, I believe that God wants something done for you, and if a believer can't or won't make it happen, He is not above moving on an unbeliever to get the job done.

CHRIST DIDN'T COME JUST TO TEACH US, HE CAME TO SHOW US A REVELATION OF LOVE AND JUSTICE

When you understand that it's the love of Christ that is guiding you, then you can feel so much more at peace with the unexpected people God uses to help you along your journey in life. When you understand that it's a form of justice in God's sight, it will bless you when you see God using the unbeliever to work out His plan for you. When you've obeyed the Lord, followed His Word and will, and are believing in faith for the answer to your prayers, it's like, even if it takes a heathen to get it done, justice will be served!

So, you can rest easy if you're obedient to God like Mary and Joseph were as they left home for Bethlehem. Just like God was using an unbeliever to get them where they needed to be, so God just may use an unbeliever to get you where you need to be! It might not be comfortable at first, and it might not even look right, but you're on the right path going to the right place to do the right thing! If your heart is right and you are following God's Word and God's lead, then don't let worry or doubt derail your faith. Your future is good!

I always make sure to keep my mindset positive—I know that my future is always going to be good because I've read the back of the Book! The Bible is my future. God Almighty loves me, sent Jesus for me, and will always be faithful to perform His Word if I do my part.

HIS PEACE, HIS REST—THE LORD LOVES US SO MUCH

If Jesus tarries and I die, I know that even my death will be a good one! God will never leave me or forsake me—so if I die before Jesus comes back, I know that God will be right there just like He was right there when I was born. God loves us! Do you understand how much He loves us?

His love and justice will prevail in all areas. I love when Jesus said, "My peace I give unto you" because I don't have to rely on my own peace—I rely on His peace. When my time comes, I will "enter into the rest of the Lord" like the scripture says too. Again, it's not my rest; it's His rest I'll be entering into. In other words, Heaven! What a restful place. What a comfort!

When Jesus ascended, He promised to send the Holy Spirit down—another way He showed us that He'd never leave us or forsake us. The Holy Spirit is called "the Comforter" for a reason. We will need His comfort sometimes more than others, and it's good to know that He is always nearby and waiting, ready to comfort our heart and lift us up!

GOD DOESN'T AVOID THE UGLY PLACES THAT THE DEVIL ONCE TROD

I believe that God can and will use even the biggest heathen in this world if that's what it takes to perform His Word to you. They'll likely be like Caesar Augustus and not even realize they are being used, but that doesn't matter.

You know, in Rome, long ago, they built those great roads so that they could move legions of military might in order to take over other countries—to rape, to kill, to plunder and steal just to add more power to their empire. What they didn't understand was that one day God would use those same roads. He'd put Paul the apostle on them and use them to bring the Gospel to the world.

Paul walked those same old roads that brought harm to so many people. God used those same highways that once supported men with nothing but conquering on the mind to bring the greatest love story ever told to mankind. Jesus' name was spoken on those same roads. People got born again and filled with the spirit on those roads.

Don't think that God avoids the ugly places that devils once trod…no, He turns the tables and takes what the devil meant for harm and turns it around for good. That is what God does. He can turn anything around! He can use anybody He wants! All we have to do is open our mind enough to see it as a good thing—a needful thing at times—and just praise God at His amazing and sometimes unusual way of getting His Word fulfilled.

Unbelievers will think that what they are doing is for their own benefit—but God is moving them so that *you* will be in the position you need to be. Unbelievers will assume that only they are benefiting from their decisions—but it is *you* who will benefit most in the end. Accept that as true, because it is. Believe it in your heart and just be amazed when you see things fall into place.

Sometimes it gets intense, I know. Let it get intense! You have the Comforter with you; don't forget. You have God watching out for you, and you can handle anything that comes your way. So, watch and wait! The unconscious obedience of the unbeliever is a mysterious thing—but when it's happening on your behalf, it's a powerful thing to see.

SOMETIMES UNBELIEVERS HATE YOU…AND STILL HELP YOU!

I can't tell you how many times unbelievers have stepped in to help me and literally told me they didn't know why they were even doing it. Sometimes they can even get nasty and say mean things; yet they will still do it! This used to bother me a little until I understood "the unconscious obedience of the unbeliever" principle.

Unbelievers will come up to me in restaurants and tell me they don't believe in God, but they watch me on television. They'll hand me money for the ministry and walk off nearly angry at themselves for doing it. God's work needs doing. I know it and God knows it, and it's almost funny to me now the way He will move on people to fund His work.

It even sometimes helps me personally. I remember once I left my hotel to walk around the city I was in before going to the convention center for a meeting. I got really thirsty and went into a convenience store, but it wasn't until I was standing in front of the drinks that I realized I'd forgotten my wallet in the room. "Oh well," I thought, "I guess I'm going to have to do without."

This guy walked up to me right then and said, "Are you that preacher on television? That white-headed preacher?" He was sneering when he asked me, and so I tried to make a little joke to lighten it up. In my most dignified voice, I said, "Yes, I'm Robert Schuler, how are you doing?" I was trying to be nice, you know, even though I could tell he didn't like me.

You know, I'm always amazed that if you are on television or the web, people feel like they can say any old mean thing to you and it's OK. The man looked me up and down and said, "Well, I ain't into the God stuff. I don't believe anything you say."

"Well," I said, "I believe everything I say!" and I smiled at him.

He said, "You look like you're happy about it."

I said, "I certainly am."

"What are you doing here?" he asked.

I didn't want to tell him I was thirsty but had forgotten my wallet, so I told him the other truth about why I was out and about. "Well," I said, "uhhh…I just walked here from the hotel, ummmm, you know, just to see things. I don't get a chance to see much of anything other than a church or convention center, so I just thought I'd see a few things."

"Well, you know, like I said…I ain't into the God stuff. You thirsty? I want a real drink. You probably don't drink, but you might want a Coke or something. Right?" he asked.

I said, "You know, I believe the Lord is telling you to do that."

He said, "Well, I tell ya what…I ain't never bought a preacher a Coke in my life, but I'm buying one today."

I made another joke. "Be careful," I said, "God might make you give me a two-liter and not just a…." and he interrupted me.

"Whoa, I never thought of it like that, but well, I don't know!" he said, clearly thinking about the idea that God might use him to help a preacher like me that he didn't even like.

It was so simple, I know. It's no big deal at all. Ahhhh, but I was thirsty! And there he was, helping me. Now, it may seem small and it is small, but God says He notices even the sparrows. So, He must see all the little things as well as the big ones. Sometimes I think the little blessings can sometimes feel the best.

I LOVE WHEN GOD GOES OUT OF HIS WAY TO MAKE ME FEEL LOVED

When the media attacks me for believing in abundance, I always feel the backlash when I go out in public—but what amazes me is that, in those times, I also feel the immense love of people too. It's like people come out of the woodwork just to tell me how much they love the ministry or how much something I've said has helped them turn their lives around.

Sometimes, after the media really attacks, I'll meet unbelievers on the street who tell me they don't believe in God but they like me. In the same breath that they tell me they don't believe, they'll also tell me they watch my program once a week. Some will run up to me on the street after seeing bad press, pat me on the back, or hug my neck and holler, "Fake news! Don't let it get you down!" Some will just hand me twenty dollars and say, "Ahhhh, you can't believe anything the news says. Look, I'm an atheist, but put that in your ministry!" It's gotten funny how often that kind of thing happens.

And with the believers, it's like the testimonies escalate right in tandem with the attacks of the devil. I think it's God's way of reminding me not to get tunnel-visioned listening to those who hate God or my ministry. It's such a blessing to hear that people's lives have been changed by the power of God. I know mine has, and when I preach I hope that God's Word helps others, too. When they tell me testimonies of their salvation or healing, or how they got out of debt, or how God supernaturally blessed their finances, I always walk away feeling so grateful that God would move upon people to say such kind things to me, especially in those times. I also feel so loved that people would be willing to stick their neck out and take the heat for showing me kindness in public, too. It's such a blessing.

God sends people along our path, you know. Some bless us, some curse us, and some physically help us or encourage us in some way. God can use *anybody* to help fulfill His plan in our own lives and in this world. Don't forget it!

Remember Caesar Augustus when you're looking at your life and wondering how God is ever going to bring His promise to pass for you. Remember that he was one of the players in God's big plan for mankind—and if Caesar hadn't wanted his tax money, there would have never been a census, and there would have been no good reason to get Joseph and Mary to Bethlehem. A trip on the back of a donkey might not have been comfortable or preferable, and it sure didn't look right. But God was working, and He made sure Jesus was right where He needed to be in the end—fulfilling the old prophecy and bringing new promise to the whole wide world in the process.

God moves in mysterious ways and sometimes blessings come disguised. The unconscious obedience of unbelievers is just one of those unusual ways God sometimes works—I hope you never forget it!

John the Baptist

GOD ALWAYS SENDS A FORERUNNER

Chapter 5

John the Baptist—The Forerunner
to Jesus' First Coming

When angels get excited about something, you know it's something *big*. Messengers of God act as servants to God—but we are sons and daughters of God, and there is a vast difference between a son and a servant. One is born of God. The other is not. When the original scripture talks about us, it tells us that we have been made a little lower than God—but the translators couldn't handle that. They believed it was too much and put the word *angels* in the translation instead, deliberately getting it wrong because who could say such a thing? And what would it mean if we believed such a thing? Yet that is the Word of God, and God means what He said. He created us a little lower than Himself, on purpose for a purpose.

We are the supreme creation of God Almighty on this earth, and in Heaven as well—and that's one reason why Satan hates mankind so much. He was made beautiful, powerful, and high in rank among the angels, and he was created before us. And yet God made us his boss. Adam had more authority than Satan, even though he submitted to Satan by his own free will. He did not have to do it; Adam chose to do it because he believed the lie Satan fed him.

Satan hated Adam and he hates all of Adam's seed too—he will use us, abuse us, and do everything he can to steal, kill, and destroy us. Why? Because he resents us. Pride caused him to fall, and pride keeps him working toward destroying the ones God loves—us, the ones God calls His children. Jesus redeemed us and made a way back for us, and He has given us the authority to use His name. This is why Satan can't win. He can fight. He can hinder. We can submit to him and let him take us for a ride. But when we know who we are, where we come from, and the power that has been given to us as sons and daughters of God…well, Satan knows that he cannot win, no matter how hard he tries.

John the Baptist was a powerhouse of a man who did not flinch when it came to Satan—in fact, he didn't bother talking about him that much at all. John had authority. He knew who he was and why he was on the earth. John was a forerunner to Jesus Christ.

Do not be deceived into thinking that you are on this planet haphazardly. Just like God sent John the Baptist into the world six months ahead of Jesus on purpose, you were placed on the earth at the time you were born for a purpose.

John's calling was to draw attention to the One. His birth and life were unusual and marked by the power of the Holy Spirit. John was fiery preacher and a bold man. God gave him the disposition for the calling he was destined to fulfill.

Many say that John the Baptist was the greatest preacher who ever lived. After all, if God chooses you to be the opening man for Christ, well, you've got to be anointed. John could preach hell so hot, you'd swear you could smell the smoke! He was totally unique and utterly different from anybody who came before him talking about God.

John the Baptist had *zero* miracles in his ministry. None whatsoever! Yet the whole city would follow him out into the wilderness just to hear him preach. What made John so great? Many things! Here's one: John knew and understood his position.

John knew what God called him to do, and that was to proclaim the coming of the Messiah. He did not ignore his calling or second-guess the words he knew he had to say, and he did not compromise or flinch in the face of Satan or powerful people in his day. John spoke the truth, and he didn't soften it very much at all! That was the kind of man God chose to cut the path for Jesus to come.

Let me ask you a question: Do you understand your position? The Christmas story shows us that whenever Jesus is about to come on the scene, God uses unbelievers in unusual ways to get people into place. He gives planetary and star signs in the heavens and unusual natural phenomenon on the earth, and most importantly to me—God sends forerunners. I believe that *we* are forerunners!

God strategically placed people on the earth right before Jesus came. He will do the same right before Jesus comes back, and I believe Jesus is coming a lot sooner than people think. Forerunners are bold. Forerunners are fearless in the face of opposition and satanic forces. Forerunners do not cower or flinch but herald the coming of purity by speaking pure words of truth—even if they are hard to hear. John was just such a man!

ELISABETH:
BARREN, MENOPAUSAL, AND PREGNANT
ZACHARIAS:
SCARED, DOUBTFUL, AND SPEECHLESS

Elisabeth had been barren her whole life—and the scripture begins her story when she's past menopause and knows that she is doubly incapable of having children. Now, this woman hoped for children when she was younger. She'd prayed for children even as she got older. Everybody in town knows that it's just not possible for Elisabeth, except for God, Who doesn't care about the word *impossible*. This is the woman God chose to be the mother of John the Baptist.

Zacharias was Elisabeth's husband. He was from one of the priestly families and the scripture tells us that both of them were righteous before God and walked in all the commandments and ordinances of God without failing. Way back before he was born, King David and Samuel had split the priests into twenty-four orders or courses, because there were so many priests and they couldn't all serve at the same time. This gave everyone a chance to serve. After the Babylonians conquered, there were only four orders left, but King Ezra wanted to establish the twenty-four groups again, so he split up the four and that's where Zacharias came in. The priests all left their houses and wives behind to serve one week two times a year, from Sabbath to Sabbath, and it was during this time that Zacharias got the shock of his life. What happened left him altogether speechless. Listen to this!

One day, Zacharias was going to light the incense in the temple, which was occasionally one of his duties, so that the people could offer sacrifices and pray. When he went into the temple, Zacharias suddenly was looking into the face of an angel who was standing on the right side of the altar—exactly where he was supposed to light the incense. Zacharias was shocked. Luke 1:12 says that the sight of God's angel shook him up so much that pure fear just fell on him. It's not every day you see an angel on the job, even if you work at a temple.

The angel said, *"Fear not, Zacharias: for thy prayer is heard; and thy wife Elisabeth shall bear thee a son, and thou shalt call his name John"* (verse 13). Like Jesus' mother would soon experience, God chose Zacharias and Elisabeth's boy's name. Remember, John is forerunner.

The angel continued, *"And thou shalt have joy and gladness; and many shall rejoice at his birth"* (verse 14). The angel is confirming that John is going to make both of them so happy, and even those around town who know their struggles in conceiving are going to cheer when John is born into the world.

Next, the angel prepares Zacharias for the type of man his son will one day be saying, *"For he shall be great in the sight of the Lord, and shall drink neither wine nor strong drink; and he shall be filled with the Holy Ghost, even from his mother's womb"* (verse 15). God literally thinks of John in terms of greatness—John is going to do some amazing things, and to do them, his life is going to be marked by purity and fiery spirituality. John will be an eyes-wide-open kind of man, and he will care what he puts into his own body.

No wine and no strong drink—John the Baptist is going to be supernaturally filled with the Holy Spirit before he is even finished being fully formed in his mother's womb. This is a man who is going to prepare the way for Jesus, and he is going to be eagle-eyed looking for the Christ—he will not cloud his vision with anything. He will keep his body clean so it is performing at its best. He will lean on the Holy Spirit, be a keen observer, and do great things in God's eyes.

Now remember, the Holy Spirit hadn't fallen in the upper room—none of that had occurred yet—so, John would be a forerunner for the baptism of the Holy Spirit too. God knew that John would need the boldness and purity of the Holy Spirit in order to fulfill his calling.

What we have to do requires the Holy Spirit too, and it's available to us all today, but in John's time the Holy Spirit was not so readily accessible. I want you to see that God gives us what we need *inside* to do what we are meant to do, including you and me. Our nature actually supports our calling. John's calling required boldness and intensity and the ability to live outside of the norms of that day—to be a purist in spirit, in body, and in speech. John would be a man who didn't mince words. Unlike his father, which we will get to in a moment, John would not be double-minded; he would not waste time going back and forth with God but instead would be quick to believe, quick to obey, and quick to speak what the Spirit led him to say. Again, John's nature would support his calling, but God knew John needed more than his nature—so he gave John a dose of the Holy Ghost to kick his nature up even further.

The angel continues, *"And many of the children of Israel shall he turn to the Lord their God. And he shall go before Him in the spirit and power of Elias, to turn the hearts of the fathers to the children"* (verses 16-17). So, John is going to affect people spiritually and physically—yet he will have no miracles in his ministry. But with the Holy Spirit and the words he speaks, he will have the ability to influence men so that their hearts are opened to their own children. So, John will be a proponent of the family man. He will be a champion of the father/child relationship. Again, forerunner!

God is interested in fathers because He is the Father. God was about to send His only child, His Son, to the world. So, part of John's calling was to stir up the masculine heart and influence men—he was going to speak in a way that propelled the bridging of gaps between fathers and their children. Forerunner!

I believe that if God did this before the first coming, He is going to do this before the second coming. Strong men, bold men, and unflinchingly honest, spirit-filled men are going to pop up before the second coming—watch for it! Why do you think the devil is so intent in this day and age on tearing men down, feminizing men, and demonizing masculinity? Satan is afraid of godly men. He didn't even have the guts to go at Adam straightforward but instead targeted his wife as a way to bring them both down. Satan is an angelic coward.

Then the angel said John would also be a forerunner in turning *"the disobedient to the wisdom of the just,"* which means John was going to plow the field of foolishness out in the world during his time. He was going to take the rampant disobedience and start preaching with such wisdom and clarity that everybody would understand what was wrong and right in God's sight. The angel was warning John's daddy ahead of time that John's life would be marked by masculine, God-centered love of what was right.

What was the purpose of this kind of personality and the infilling of the Holy Spirit? The angel said John would be that way for this reason: *"to make **ready** a people **prepared** for the Lord."* John's job was to get the people ready. His job was to prepare them for Jesus. I am convinced that God will do similar things as the second coming approaches—He will make sure people hear what they need to get ready. Whether they accept it is up to them, but they will hear.

Zacharias heard all of this and do you know how he responded? He literally told the angel to give him a sign—and then he gave the angel an excuse about why it couldn't happen. Can you imagine? *"And Zacharias said unto the angel, Whereby shall I know this? for I am an old man, and my wife well stricken in years"* (verse 18).

It's almost funny. The man is looking square at a huge angel and he wants more signs! Then, he thinks, "Eeeeeh, I don't know about this. How am I going to know that's true? That's not possible, my wife and I are just plain old." The angel doesn't play around. He's got a woman named Mary to meet next and he's not going to play around with this doubting priest while the Son of God's mama is waiting. I like that the angel tells him his name, as in, "Uh, do you know who I am and Who sent me? I came to give you good news! But, here you are—you don't believe anything! God sent me, man, and now you gonna have to shut up!" That's exactly what happened, you know. Go ahead, read it in Luke 1:19-20 for yourself.

> *And the angel answering said unto him, I am Gabriel, that stand in the presence of God; and am sent to speak unto thee, and to shew thee these glad tidings. And, behold, thou shalt be dumb, and not able to speak, until the day that these things shall be performed, because thou believest not my words, which shall be fulfilled in their season.*

Meanwhile, everybody who is coming to the temple is wondering what in the world is taking Zacharias so long to light the incense! They are outside thinking, "Good Lord, how long does it take?" And, when he finally comes out, guess what? He can't tell them! He is literally speechless, and everybody then assumes he has seen a vision of some kind and is in a state of spiritual ecstasy.

Zacharias finishes his time of performing priestly functions and then returns home, still not being able to talk—but he is able to do *other* things. Within days, Elisabeth conceives John the Baptist, and Zacharias remains completely speechless until the day John is born. Now, let's get into some more of what John's coming means for us today. What made John so "great" to God?

Chapter 6

What Made John Great in God's Sight Will Make You Great in His Sight, Too

The first person to preach the Gospel was John the Baptist— the Gospel required a forerunner. Until John the Baptist started preaching, many people believed in the Messiah but they never thought in terms of "the Son of God." So, John was not only a forerunner of Jesus Himself, but he was also the forerunner of the message itself. What made God call John's actions great? What made John a great man to God? One word: obedience!

Do you obey what the Lord tells you to do? John wasn't unusual because God had a plan for his life—God has a plan for all of our lives. What was unusual was that John was the "preparing one" for Jesus' first time on the earth. That was new. But the fact that there was a plan and a calling on his life—that wasn't a new concept at all. God's Word tells us that He knows us before we are even formed in our mother's womb—*before*. God knew John before Elisabeth was even pregnant, and He knew you before your mama was pregnant, too.

You are a spirit, you have a soul, and you are housed in a body. The last thing you are is a body, and that's the only thing that's going when you die. So, you were *known* before and you will be *known* after. Your time here on earth is precious to God, and you are going to make an impact in some area or another—you were born to, and if you stick with God, you will. Obedience will help you on this journey.

You see, John was great because he was obedient to his life's calling, and when it comes to you, you just have to know that your life has already been a thought in the mind of God. So, if you want to fulfill your purpose, you have to move in the direction God reveals to you and that requires what? Obedience. Sometimes it's not a grandiose, revelatory plan. Some seem to know more than others, but often you will just plain need to live step-by-step by faith. You take one step, God shows you the next. You consult the Holy Spirit within you. You take the next step.

Greatness in God's eyes is always marked by obedience—because obeying Him is in your best interests. We must do what God wants all of the time, and on time. If God quickens your heart to give something to someone, don't sit around wrestling with the idea—just do it. You have no earthly idea what your obedience means to the person God puts on your heart. You do not know the ripple effects. Sometimes the simplest things God asks us to do, we don't do because we think they don't matter. If the Holy Spirit prompts you—it matters.

OVERTHINKING AND OBEDIENCE DON'T MIX

Many times people tell me, "God told me this" or "God told me to do that" and then they ask, "What do you think?" I nearly want to laugh. Are you kidding me? Who cares what I think! God told you to do something! You don't need advice; you need to obey what He said to you.

Some people will say, "God told me to do this" and then they'll turn around and say, "I'm going to pray about it." What? Pray about it? God told you to do it; do you think He's going to change His mind? Or are you just giving yourself time to stall long enough to squash down His voice in your own heart? Just go do it.

Jesus tells us that He is the Good Shepherd and we are His sheep and we know His voice. Most of the time when people wrestle with something God is leading them to do, they are really just wondering if it will work or if it's the right thing to do. They start wondering how they are going to make something happen—which is just making their own abilities their source. God is our Source, and if He prompts us to do something, we will not be left high and dry doing it alone. He is with us. He will provide for us. The more faith we have in Him and the quicker we'll do what He said, the greater the reward for doing it. It's in our best interests to obey God.

The angel's response to Zacharias shows us that overthinking and obedience don't mix—when we do that, it just slows the wheels of progress and it irritates even angels! Just do what God said.

IF YOU KNOW GOD SAID IT, WHY DO YOU "HAVE TO PRAY ABOUT IT"?

In the Church we have a lot of little slogans we use to avoid doing what God says—and the most common one I hear is, "I'll have to pray about that." If God tells me to do something, I immediately go do it. I don't go pray about it; I do it. I recognize that sometimes I don't *want* to do it, but I've decided that obedience to God's Word or what He has told me to do is more valuable to me than comfort.

It's comfortable to stay the same. Sometimes even the bad things get so comfortable, people stay there just because they don't want the discomfort of change or obedience to God.

I've developed a good relationship with God and I know when He tells me to do something. More than once, when I've let myself slide into reasoning with myself or overthinking what He's said because it seems like too much, He has told me things like, "If you don't want to do this, I'll get somebody else who will." *Whoa!* God has told me to give away large sums of money many times—sometimes amounts that I'd been saving for something else. But He told me to sow it, and I didn't just hesitate—I did a looong pause. I'll tell you, I wanted to go "pray about it!"

God will challenge my long pauses! He knows just what to say to me to get me to a place of either choosing obedience or disobedience. After mulling something over too long, I remember trying to get Him to understand by saying, "God, I didn't say I *wasn't* going to do it…I'm just thinking about it here!" I remember Him telling me, "That's your problem. You're thinking too long. I've already thought about it. Now you go and do what I said."

God wants us to do what He said all the time and on time—which means quickly, before we talk ourselves out of a good thing.

Tough as a Corncob, but Quick to Obey

I've met very few people in my life who are quick to obey. One of the greatest men I ever met had a quick-to-obey and quick-to-move mentality when it came to the things of God. He was a little rough! He was as rough as a corncob, to tell you the truth—and I found that in the same way he was quick to obey God, he was quick to eat your lunch, so to speak, if you floundered too long. His name was Lester Sumrall, and although he's in Heaven now, I'll never forget the first time he called me and invited me to preach for him. The conversation went like this:

"Jesse Duplantis?"

"Yes, this is Jesse."

"This is Lester Sumrall."

"Hello, Brother Sumrall! How are you doing?"

"I'm doing good," he said, "Listen, I want you to come preach at my camp meeting."

"Well, Brother Sumrall, praise God! Let me look at my calendar and I'll pray about it."

He said, "I already prayed."

I didn't know what to say to that and I guess I paused too long.

"You think I'd call you without praying? Why do you have to pray about it? You believe I'm a man of God?"

"Yes!" I said, "Yes, I do!"

"Then, why are you praying about it? You think I'd call you without praying?"

Man, I was searching for words to say!

"Well, Brother Sumrall, I guess I don't have to," I said.

"See?" he said, "You don't have to! When are you coming?"

"I'm loaded up right now; I can't come at this time," I said, knowing that his camp meeting was coming up and I was already booked that week.

"God didn't tell me when you were coming; He just told me that you were coming."

You see, Lester was the kind of man who was quick to obey. If God told him I'd come, he picked up the phone to make the call and get the ball rolling. He didn't waste time thinking about it or praying about it, and he wouldn't let you do much of that either.

"I'll come next year then," I said.

He said, "Good! We'll have a good time. May the Lord richly bless you!" and then he just hung up.

I put it in my calendar and that was that. Our staff took over from there with the logistics, but the event was set in stone.

I never forgot that call because it was so unusual to me—usually preachers don't talk like that, and most Christians don't either. God talks like that to me, though. He didn't always, but as I grew and developed as a believer, and as I stretched my faith, He put the pressure on my obedience. He will bring me to a point of choice quick nowadays! No mulling it over forever. It's my job to either do it immediately if I can or put my faith on it to immediately start the process of drawing in what He has said.

I consider obedience the main reason why I've been blessed financially—I'm a tither, I'm a giver, and when God tells me to bless someone, fund something, or sow a certain amount, well, I do it. I'm quick to do it. I don't just preach this; I live it. Obedience giving is part of who I am. If I know that I've heard the voice of God, I just know that I must do what He said at the time He said it, and on time—and I know that He will bless me in return beyond what I can think or imagine. I truly believe I cannot out-give God.

GREATNESS IN GOD'S SIGHT IS WITHIN THE REACH OF ALL

John the Baptist didn't look that great—he never wore a tie or even the nice things of that day, but God said he *was* great. God does not care what we look like, but He cares very much about the condition of our heart. John wore something so odd, the scriptures recorded it! The man wore camel hair skins with a big leather belt—he lived a self-imposed austere lifestyle and ate a diet of locusts and wild honey.

Now, there is debate about just what a locust was, but most believe it was definitely not the bug since John was known for not eating any kind of flesh. So, it was either the bean pods from the local carob trees that were shaped a little like a locust or a honey cake made from local wild vegetation that some ate because it resembled manna.

Either way, bean pod or vegetable cake, John was definitely living his own way and abstaining from all sorts of things—from meat, to bread, to wine, hard liquor, and even some people. John was living like a vegan loner out in the wilderness. When he wasn't preaching, he chose a solitary life, and I believe it was in those solitary times that God gave him the revelations he needed to cut the path for Jesus Christ.

Do you have to buy some camel hair clothes? Start eating vegan? Move out to the wilderness? Do you have to do any of that to be "great" in God's eyes? No—you are already great in God's eyes. Jesus has washed you clean and redemption has changed the whole situation. You just need to start seeing yourself for who you really are in Christ so that you take on the position you've been given.

You are blessed in the city, blessed in the field, blessed coming in, and blessed going out, in God's eyes. You are already healed from the top of your head to the bottom of your feet, in God's eyes. You see, if you start seeing yourself the way God sees you, through the blood of Jesus, then you're gonna really be a great forerunner for the second time He comes around. All you have to do is renew your mind to the Word so you can think God's way and accept who you really are in Him—and then, when God says to do something, do it! Follow Him step-by-step, day-by-day. Greatness is within reach for us *all*.

Don't listen to the lies that say you can't do this or that, or that you aren't good enough—you are more than good enough; you are *great* in God's eyes. Don't accept a thought that is anything less than that. You don't have to change who *you* are; you have to *be* who you really are. It's in Christ that you find your identity, not in hobbies or jobs or anything else. You cannot really know yourself outside of knowing where you came from—and that is from God. James 1:22-24 says that a person who doesn't know God is like a man who looks into a mirror to see his own reflection, but when he leaves he immediately forgets what he looks like.

Knowing that God has made you great takes the pressure off—you can now just do what He says knowing that it's in your best interests. You aren't performing for God. You're creating a future for yourself and others. You are paving the way for the return of Christ. With every word of testimony you give, you are proclaiming the goodness of God, which is spreading light in the world. With every person you affect for good, introduce to Christ, or with every good work you do, you are propelling the goodness of God in this earth. As believers, "preparing the way" is all of our jobs!

I was born in 1949. I've been preaching since 1976. I will preach until God takes me home or Jesus comes back—I will not retire because my calling doesn't have an end. I don't want to stop sowing good into this world and I don't want to stop seeing people find the Lord Jesus as their Savior. I want people to know how to use faith, think higher, and live in abundance—spiritually, physically, and financially. I want people to know that darkness has no hold over people who walk in the light, and the devil is no match for the God that we serve. I've read the back of the book and we win!

Don't look at people like they are worthless—they are *great* in God's sight. See your children through the eyes of the Lord, and notice how great they are. God chose them to come through you into this world. Do not put yourself in league with the devil by tearing down your own seed. Remember John the Baptist—remember that his ministry was to turn the heart back to the children. God wanted that, so John wanted that, too. You must want it as well. Who knows what your kids will go on to do? They might be wearing camel clothes too one day, proclaiming the coming of our Lord!

Chapter 7

The Power of
Spiritual Preparation

Spiritual preparation is so important. If you want the best things (which is God's best for your life, which includes your calling, your goals, and the desires of your heart) but you aren't "there yet," it's time to prepare for where God is taking you. Nobody else but you may see what you do, but it matters.

Preparing spiritually is laying the groundwork for where you're going. To be a forerunner, you have to run! To run, you need energy—spiritual preparation is what is going to give you the energy you need to run the race God has set before you. John prepared for the best things. He knew the importance of his own time with God, in solitude, and did it.

Today, people don't prepare for the best things because they don't realize they need to—they assume that everything will just "happen" as it is supposed to, or they will wing it as they move through life. Spiritual preparation is about honoring God now, praying now, reading the Word—changing the random thoughts of the mind into the disciplined thoughts of a well-trained mind.

Work backward if you need to. Think of what you'll be doing. What kind of habits does a person doing *that* live out each day? John knew he needed to hear from the Holy Spirit within him— even though he was filled from his mother's womb, he still had to dedicate himself to praying in the Holy Spirit, jumping to obey the promptings of the Spirit, and filling his mind with the Word of God. God gave him the nature and the gift, but he still had to act upon what he'd been given.

So, realize you need to prepare yourself for that best life now—in your mind, in the words that you are saying about yourself and God, and in the small actions you take every single day. Athletes train to be the best at what they do. John was a spiritual powerhouse who took his spiritual training seriously.

I'm sure John didn't love the wilderness all the time—hot air and sandy food! But I believe that he saw that place as critical for keeping himself on target with his calling. It was extreme. But, for him, it was the preparation he needed to do what God called him to do. To be the man God wanted him to be, he had to live his life accordingly. John was not escaping life—a lot of Christians use prayer to escape. John was preparing for life. The Way, the Truth, and the Life was about to be revealed through him—and although he was bold, brash, and a powerful speaker, John knew that time in the wilderness alone was the atmosphere necessary for him.

What did Paul do when he went into the ministry? He went into the Arabian Desert. What was he doing? He was preparing himself spiritually for what he had to do. You see, a lot of people don't realize that they even need to prepare, so they allow distractions to rob them of their preparation time. You cannot give what you don't have—but quiet time alone with God will fuel you for whatever is coming next.

In all areas of life, successful people prepare for what they want to do—but it is especially needful for believers. Our preparation is about prayer, the Word, and changing the way we think to match God's way of thinking. It's the fuel that propels our actions. All of us are called to change the world by bringing the message of Christ to people. We are not all John the Baptists, but we all have something we are meant to do to affect others for good—and that work requires that we prepare our hearts and minds. The real work is the work that begins with ourselves. Prepare for your calling every day. Consider it sowing seeds toward the good future in store for you. The bonus of preparing is the joy it gives you that day and the ability to be "instant in season and out" in the future.

YOUR FAITH INFLUENCES OTHERS— IF YOU DON'T SPEAK, EARS WON'T HEAR

People can't hear what we don't say—so if we don't speak faith, others won't hear faith. Faith is lost when there is spiritual silence. We cannot just assume that people know. As believers, we must share what we've been given. We need to see ourselves as forerunners for Jesus. If He were coming back tomorrow, would you tell somebody about Him today? Would you share your testimony? Would you tell the story of what He has done in your life?

When God sent John the Baptist as a forerunner, He sent a bold man who spoke the truth—it was more extreme than we see today, but it was necessary. He was the man who needed to cut that field, so to speak, and plow the way for Jesus. People have acted similarly throughout human history. The same heart level problems exist today that existed in John and Jesus' time—because the devil has no new tricks!

John the Baptist was not afraid to say what needed to be said, even if it smacked right up against the powers of the day. He told King Herod Antipas that he was an adulterer—and while it was dangerous to speak like that, John believed that the truth had to be said and without softening it. His message was continually, "Repent, for the kingdom of God is at hand!" That is what God had sent him to say, so repentance from sin was extremely important to him. John had a very clear view of the deception of sin and wanted people to be free.

John didn't care if you were rich, powerful, and held public office. He didn't care if you had nothing at all. He spoke the truth and influenced others to prepare their hearts for the coming of the Messiah. He refused to be silent about it, and yet he preached in the wilderness. Mobs of people were drawn to hear "the voice of one crying in the wilderness."

The fire of the Holy Spirit that caused him to live such a pure life also brought the heat to everybody who had the guts to go out there and listen. Lives were changed forever, and even Jesus respected John so much that He asked him to baptize Him in the river.

When the Son of God asks you to pray over Him, you know you're doing something right! God couldn't help Himself and hollered down, "This is My Son in whom I am well pleased!" In other words, "That's My Boy! I'm so proud of Him!" So, God was at the meeting in the wilderness when John was preaching. And God was at the baptism in the river! God showed up when John talked—God always shows up when we flow in His Holy Spirit. Where two or more are gathered in His name, He is *there* in the midst of us. Glory!

You Should Grow Thick Skin, but Not a Hard Heart

Most people cower in the face of power, but not John the Baptist. He loved truth more than his own life, and he was willing to take the heat for what he believed. Are you?

If you "bring the heat," so to speak, you've also got to be able to take the heat! The Holy Spirit can help you—it is literally what brings the boldness to witness. It will help you witness for Christ, and it will help you to be a witness in whatever you do. It also draws its share of faith-haters!

People with no vision will always try and stamp out yours. People who live in fear always want to control those who live in faith. So what! See that junk for what it is—fear and limitation. Let people do what they need to do. You just stick to your calling, your vision, your goals, and the desires God has placed on your heart. Don't waste your time worrying about the opinions of others.

People have fought my ministry for years—they've said all kinds of lies about me and twisted my own words to suit their idea of just who they think I am. It hurts, but I can't be moved. If God told me to believe for something, then I'm going to have faith in what He said—not what other people say! If God revealed something I know will help others, I have to share it. I can't be deterred by what some other person likes or doesn't like—and I don't care if they work for the news networks!

The truth is that if you want to obey God, you will have to grow some thick skin. I didn't say a hard heart! Thick skin isn't a hard heart. It's about valuing what God said more than what anybody else said. Nobody saved you but God. Give God His due! Respect Him enough to choose His Word over everybody else's words.

You have to just accept that people will not always understand what you're doing if you're following God's plan for your life, but that's OK. God didn't tell them; He told you! They've got their own plan. Good! Bless them and wish them well, pray for them and let their words go—good or bad, let their words go.

You have all the support you need in God. Know it! Your family may not support you. Your kids may criticize you. If you gain traction and see success and others find out, even people you don't know may cut your guts out with their words. So what! They are not God and you don't have to bend to the pressure of a naysayer or some group who doesn't believe in God's plan for your life.

Be a leader in your own life and don't cave to that mental garbage. You can be sad about it a little while; you can be slightly disappointed. You have permission to feel whatever you feel…for a short while! Don't let that drag out if you know what's good for you. Remind yourself Who you serve and who you are! Whether they like you or not is irrelevant; that does not change what God said. God loves you. You know that! Love yourself too. Say good things about yourself to yourself—just drown them out in your own head.

I promise there will be people who will love seeing you be a forerunner, fulfilling God's plan in your life. So, do your thing! Run your race. Be the forerunner for Jesus' next coming, even if you sell cars for a living. Sell as many cars as you can. Believe God to outsell yourself every other day! Maybe you'll own a car lot, fund the Gospel, and bless people with good cars that they need to get where they want to go.

See whatever you are doing as a ministry of sorts—helping people is what it is all about. Speaking faith while you are helping people—that is when you become an even a greater influence. Again, they cannot hear what you do not speak. So speak! Let the Holy

Spirit be ever present so that you say something good. You may be quiet or you may be bold. You may be dressed one way or another. The externals matter to you and others too, but they don't matter to God—it's your message that matters. What are you saying?

John the Baptist shows us that in order to be a truth-speaker, you must walk the walk! You cannot just talk to the talk. With the same measure you judge others, that is the measurement that will be used to judge you—which means, before you say something, you better be clean! There's a reason why John was so bold. He was living his purest life, with the Holy fire of God burning in his heart—and he became known as "the one crying out in the wilderness" with a message that drew people to him like magnets.

People need God. They are looking for authenticity. Will they find it in you? They should! I promise, the ones who are affected for good through your life are worth the price of all the spiritual preparation you are doing—lives will be changed through you, through the goals and visions you have, and through your influence. Your life is talking. Make sure others are hearing something good!

Chapter 8

You Can't Live Two Lives Any More Than You Can Serve Two Masters

I was such a good sinner before I got saved. I drank a lot of booze; I was a very heavy drinker. Once I got born again, I was set free. I didn't want it. I had something so much better inside of me—Jesus—and I literally felt on top of the world.

You see, when He forgave me, I forgave myself. I allowed that forgiveness, that grace and mercy, to flow not just over me but inside of me. I released everything I had to Him and I just never looked back. In my mind, there was no place to go back to. I'd done it all, seen it all, and drank it all—it couldn't give me what I really needed. Jesus gave me what I needed.

So when I started going to church and shared my testimony, I was shocked when preachers would warn me, "Stay away from people who drink booze because you had a problem with that." Or when they heard I used to run around with women all the time before I got saved, they'd warn, "Stay away from women, you know you used to have a problem with that." The funny thing is that they'd want to hear my old sinner stories; they would ask me for them—and that's when I knew. I didn't have a problem, *they* did. They wanted to live two lives.

When I got saved, I gave up that old life—because it wasn't worth keeping. I gained a new life, and it was not hard for me to be a Christian or to be moral. It wasn't hard for me to pass up whiskey, even though I used to drink a fifth of it a day. Old things had passed away from me. I saw the old clubs I used to play rock music in for what they were—velvet sewers. I didn't want it anymore.

What were those preachers doing? They were continuing to judge my new holy life by my old sinful life! They just assumed that if I would fall for booze as a sinner that I'd fall for it as a Christian, too—but I had been saved too deeply for that. I couldn't live two lives any more than I could serve two masters!

You see, once you do every sin you ever wanted to do, and you find Jesus, all that sin loses its glitter. I was a rocker, and my whole life was booze, drugs, sex, and music. Been there, done that—I don't want that any more. It doesn't satisfy in the end. There must be something more. Yet the world continues to reach for that, as if wildness is some kind of good goal to have. What does it bring them in the end? Heartache, sorrow, sexually transmitted diseases, ruined livers…and for a lot of them, death too.

When I see preachers committing adultery, I get upset! We are the forerunners for the message of Christ—we are supposed to hold the standard, show the way, and help point people to Jesus. We shouldn't throw away our standards by acting just like the people we want to help. We don't need that junk. Jesus is coming—He came as a baby and He will come again to this earth. We need to see ourselves as forerunners of His return.

As believers, we need to be above the distractions of this world—our eyes must be clear so that we can see what needs to be done. We can't be in love with the sin of the world and in love with Jesus too. We have to be honest and true.

I can't wait to see what happens next when Jesus comes. I can't wait until I get to Heaven—I'm going to John the Baptist's service! I want to hear him preach some hot stuff! I want everything God has for me. So, do you think I'm going to throw all that away for some sexual fling? No woman in the world can compare to my wife or the future God has in store for me.

How do I avoid throwing it all away on something so stupid? I recognize that I must be filled with the Holy Spirit—not just on Sunday, not just a little bit, but I need to have an awareness of His presence all the time. Sin can't control me because I'm controlled by the Holy Spirit. That's where my desire to stay pure comes from. I learned it from John the Baptist!

WE ARE NOT MADE FOR COMPROMISE

John the Baptist was not made for compromise—even his parents weren't made for compromise. Zacharias may have had doubts and been dumb enough to speak them, but he wasn't a sinful man. Zacharias and Elisabeth were known as a devout and holy couple that valued the words of God. God chose John to be born to that couple for a purpose. He gave him the Holy Spirit in the womb, but it was Zacharias and Elisabeth who taught him as a child—and you better know they taught him the things of God.

They knew John was a miracle baby. They knew God had done a miracle in Elisabeth's body. The news of it made everybody they knew joyful. John was worth celebrating—and both his parents, God, and he knew that his life was meant for a whole lot more than status quo, compromised living. John had purpose.

You see, when you have purpose, it's hard to be swayed by distractions that try to pull you away from it. That's why it's so important to realize you are important! You matter. You aren't here just to eat, work, play a little, and die. You aren't here to rush through the days and race to your death. You are here to enjoy life God's way—which is the best way! Part of that is being a forerunner for His Son and being a good influence on others.

I believe in abundance. I believe in fulfilling your hopes and dreams. I believe in having everything God said you can have. But I believe that we should also be on the lookout for His appearing. Jesus is coming back, just like He said. Will He find us preparing more to meet the devil in the challenges of life than preparing to meet Him in the clouds?

God can do it all for us; we can believe for all the best things—but we must always keep His return at the deepest part of our heart. We must know that *that* is our future, and it's more important to me than anything I will ever enjoy on this planet—and I enjoy a lot of things!

We are forerunners of His return, and that always has to be close to our hearts. It is a joy to think about and also helps us to prioritize our lives so that we are reminded that it's not all about us—but it's about winning souls too, because we want as many as possible in Heaven. It's not God's will that even one person perish—He wants all to have everlasting life. That means it's our job to spread that news, to fund the Gospel, and to do what we can in our everyday lives to reach people and changes lives with the message of Jesus Christ.

WHAT YOU DEMAND FROM OTHERS YOU MUST PRACTICE YOURSELF

One of the reasons John the Baptist had an easy time telling the truth was because he was living the same truth he was preaching—and he had immediacy in his heart about the coming Christ. That is what a forerunner has in his heart. There is an urgency that helps to cut through the cobwebs.

If you knew Jesus was coming tomorrow, what would you do today? Would you live a double life tonight? If you knew He was coming, would you just surf the web or watch some TV? If you knew He was coming, what would you be thinking? Who would you be thinking about who needs to know Christ? What would you say and to whom? Think about it! What would you really *do* if you knew He was coming?

Would you argue with your wife over something stupid if you knew He was coming? Would you berate an employee or speak harshly to your own children if you knew He was coming? How would you change? What would you do? Would you fall on your face and repent, or would you shout for joy because you knew there was nothing between you and God? These are questions to ask yourself, and you can think up some more—because whatever is going on in your life right now needs to be seen through that filter of "What would you do if you *knew*?"

Jesus *is* coming and these kinds of questions can help us to snap ourselves back to where we need to be if we've lost the right attitude or the right standards for our own lives. They create urgency around what is important and what is not.

People are important, the Gospel is important, and what you say and do has the ability to turn people either *away* or *toward* Jesus Christ. If you knew He was coming, which way would you want to turn others? What kind of influence would you want to be? This is why living an authentic life as a believer is so vital. You do not have to be perfect; nobody is. But you must endeavor to walk in the truth, and speak the truth, and not cast a reflection on the beauty of what Jesus has done for humanity.

Don't ever get comfortable just spewing words—walk the walk so that you can know that you've done the best you can with the message of Christ. Don't be one of those Christians who doesn't practice what they preach, who makes the Word of God of no effect for those who hear it from their lips. If you demand something from others, you must be doing it yourself too.

As a believer, you are leading by both word and example. You can inspire people much more when they watch you *do* what you say. Don't say one thing and live another; don't demand one thing and do another—if at all possible, strive to never compromise yourself that way. It hurts not only you but all who might otherwise be influenced for good by you.

Aim to be a great forerunner for another person's salvation. Aim to cut the path that others *see* and want to follow. Let them see what God has done for you. Let them see how far He's taken you in life. Show them your blessings. Show that you've been healed. Show the smile on your face and the peace you've got in your soul. Don't just talk, *show* people the effect God has had on your life. The more honest you are about it, the more you will reach people for God and the more you will influence others for the better.

Remember that you are here on this planet to do the work and will of God, no matter what your occupation. You are designed to grow and become something greater even than you think you can be—you should be growing until you shut your eyes and go home to be with Jesus or you see Him coming in the clouds! Everything God creates is intended to grow. Challenge yourself. Don't allow yourself to get so comfortable that you give up on a better life with God. Speak well of yourself to yourself—let the Holy Spirit rise up and come out of your mouth.

You've got things to say. You've got things to do. You are a forerunner! Don't straddle the line between two lives or two masters. Don't compromise yourself or neglect to do what you tell others they should do.

Your future is depending on you, and that future includes other people who need your good influence. You've got everything you need inside of you to be the person God called you to be because you've got the Holy Spirit. Remain in a state of preparation for the second coming of the Lord and remember what made John great—obedience! John put God first. What did Jesus do? He put God first, too. All the great ones put God first. We're in this together!

I pray that you are inspired by John the Baptist to obey God, up your standards, and live the truth that you speak. If you do that, you will be known for great things because *that's* what the Holy Spirit produces. Greatness! John the Baptist had it, and I know that *you* do, too! It's *in* you—let it out for the world to see.

The Wise Men

When Science and Spirituality Converge: The Humble and Generous Magi

Chapter 9

Scientists, Worshippers, and Givers—The Wise Men Came with Their Best Intentions and Best Gifts

Their names were Melchior, Casper (or Gaspar), and Balthazar, and they were from three different places in the East—Melchior was from Persia, Casper was from India, and Balthazar was from Arabia. The Magi were called kings and wise men, and they were the scientists and diviners of that day. They were not from Israel and, yet, they were very interested in the prophecies of the Jewish people and the signs in the night sky.

Melchior, Casper, and Balthazar studied astronomy and astrology as one pursuit because at that time the two were considered inextricably linked to one another. The scientific and the spiritual? The wise men knew they were just two sides of the same coin, and they didn't consider them in opposition to each other like so many do today. Dedicated to the mathematic study of the sun, the moon, stars, planets, comets, and any other non-earthly body or phenomena in space, the wise men analyzed the changes and movement of celestial bodies—and saw some of those changes and movements as signs that could prophetically forecast earthly events.

From what they saw in the heavens, the wise men predicted that someone of royal birth had been born—and since they knew the Jewish prophecy and also King Herod, they deducted that if it wasn't Herod's child, it just might be the Christ child that the Jews had long said would one day be coming. The signs in the sky convinced them so much that they were driven to leave their own countries just to get a glimpse of who had been born. Let's look at the scripture in Matthew 2:1-12.

FINDING JESUS CAN BE TROUBLESOME TO SOME

"Now when Jesus was born in Bethlehem of Judaea in the days of Herod the king, behold, there came wise men from the east to Jerusalem, Saying, Where is He that is born King of the Jews? for we have seen His star in the east, and are come to worship Him" (verses 1-2). Notice that they were looking for a king—everything in the sky pointed to royalty, and they wanted to not only honor the new king but worship Him. Now, to say this to Herod was like saying, "Hey, you're on the way out. The Jews finally have their King; the sky is even showing that it's happened. We want to worship Him! So, where is He?"

"When Herod the king had heard these things, he was troubled, and all Jerusalem with him" (verse 3). Of course Herod was troubled—but notice that all of Jerusalem was also troubled. Satan is always troubled when Jesus shows up—and even some believers feel troubled, too.

In that day, I imagine they were thinking of what might change if the actual Messiah showed up. How would that affect them personally? What about the economy? The status quo? You'd think the people of Jerusalem would have been thrilled, but they were not—maybe, like so many people, sheer fear of the unknown was trumping any positive feelings about the future.

Desiring comfort over any kind of change, some people would rather keep the devil they know than trade him for the God they do not. The very presence of Jesus stirs up worry in some—even in the world today.

BAD RULERS DON'T CARE ABOUT YOUR FAITH OR YOUR CULTURE

When Herod asked where the child might be, the wise men gave him the answer: *"And when he had gathered all the chief priests and scribes of the people together, he demanded of them where Christ should be born. And they said unto him, In Bethlehem of Judaea: for thus it is written by the prophet"* (verses 4-5).

Notice that even though Herod ruled over the Jewish people, he wasn't interested in their culture or beliefs—bad rulers don't care about the culture or faith of others. They care about themselves alone and are only moved if it affects them personally.

Now, because it has something to do with him, Herod gets nervous. He still has no faith in those who are not directly connected to him and so, instead of relying on what the Jews or the wise men said, Herod rounds up his own people and demands an answer to the same question.

After all, what if the people want this Christ more than him? What if he's overthrown because of some prophecy? Herod starts feeling like his throne is in jeopardy—and suddenly, he starts caring about the faith hidden in the heart of the Jewish people who still believe. Satan is always shaken up by people who still believe. He doesn't care if you claim to be a Christian, so long as you don't really believe anything you claim to be true. It's true belief that shakes him up.

Herod probably thought, *If they even think it's true, I'm in trouble. If it really is true, then the Jewish God Himself is going to make a move against me from Heaven...hummmm, I got to do something about this.* Herod feels cornered.

His own people answer Herod and confirm what both the wise men said and the Jews have been saying for a long time: *"And they said unto him, In Bethlehem of Judaea, for thus it is written by the prophet: And thou Bethlehem, in the land of Juda, art not the least among the princes of Juda: for out of thee shall come a Governor, that shall rule My people Israel"* (verses 5-6). Herod then privately calls the Magi back to talk—and like the devil, he starts lying and devising a plan to deceive good people in order to take Jesus out of the picture.

"Then Herod, when he had privily called the wise men, enquired of them diligently what time the star appeared. And he sent them to Bethlehem, and said, Go and search diligently for the young child; and when ye have found Him, bring me word again, that I may come and worship Him also" (verses 7-8). Herod wants to use the wise men, not his own people—this is a tactical move. He later will make a move to kill the child, but he doesn't want anyone to know that yet, so he starts lying and acting like he wants to worship Jesus too.

The Magi are good men from a differing culture and they believe Herod's lie. The good often believe the best in even evil people—

their heart wants to believe that all have the same wish to do right, even if it isn't true. So, while the wise men likely feel wonderful being given a duty that they believe will unite everyone under a banner of worshipping God's chosen one, what is really happening is that Herod is using their good nature for his own murderous plan. The Magi are deceived and agree to do the footwork of finding Jesus, which leaves Herod looking innocent while he plans phase two.

"When they had heard the king, they departed; and, lo, the star, which they saw in the east, went before them, till it came and stood over where the young child was. When they saw the star, they rejoiced with exceeding great joy" (verses 9-10). Notice that the Magi continue to follow their original leading source of light—a "star" in the east moving south to Bethlehem.

Although the original translators chose to insert the word *star*, we also know that we get our word for planet from a Greek word that means "wandering star" too, so it has often been debated if the translators got it right since stars don't move in relation to themselves. Astronomers have been debating the realities of the "Bethlehem star" forever! But, as believers, we know that God can do anything—and whether it was a star as we know them, a moving planet, or something else entirely, the wise men were *guided* by a source of light. It is unusual to these scientists/diviners too—but they follow it. They know they are on a very unusual quest and they shout with joy when the light stops right over the house where Jesus is now living.

Unlike the typical nativities we see, Jesus is no longer in a manger. He didn't remain lacking a roof over his head. He just started there. Now, Jesus is living in a house with his mother and father. The wise men knock and they are allowed in—and it is likely a very unusual thing to Joseph and Mary, too. Here they are, men from differing cultures and likely with differing skin colors, standing at their door with precious gifts in hand. India is represented. Persia is represented. Arabia is represented. Joseph, a traditional Jew, opens the door to let them all in. There was no racism in that family. There was an openness in the heart of Joseph and Mary—they recognized the unusual realities of God's plan when it came to their Son, and they opened their house to allow others in so that they too could observe what God Himself had done through them.

"And when they were come into the house, they saw the young child with Mary His mother, and fell down, and worshipped Him: and when they had opened their treasures, they presented unto Him gifts; gold, and frankincense, and myrrh. And being warned of God in a dream that they should not return to Herod, they departed into their own country another way" (verses 11-12). The Magi were worshippers and givers—they brought their best intentions and their best gifts. At Christmastime, we follow their example with those we love, giving gifts to one another in honor of the greatest Gift God gave to mankind—Jesus Christ.

THE HUMBLE AND TEACHABLE MAGI— THE SPIRITUAL AND SCIENTIFIC CONVERGE AT THE SIGHT OF JESUS

Today, science and religion have split to such a degree that to be a person of scientific learning and a believer in God is virtually unheard of—those who are both are often ridiculed as if a mind for science and a heart for faith can't coincide. I believe that they can. I believe that science is the handmaiden of religion. I love when I see people with scientific minds who are humble and teachable in spirit. The arrogant immediately claim atheism, but you don't have to become atheistic just because you study or love science. I believe that God loves when we are fascinated by the earth and beyond—we are exploring His creation, and I believe He likely enjoys seeing us dumbfounded by His work.

The Magi were scientists of their day, and yet they were so teachable and humble that they traveled to find out if what they believed they were seeing was actually true. They wanted to know where the star led. They loved the study of the stars and planets—it wasn't just their life's work but it was a calling God had placed on their lives. I do not believe it was by accident that God drew these three scientific minds to worship His Son and to have it documented in the scripture for all of us to be reminded that, when looking in the face of Jesus Christ, the scientific and the spiritual intertwine.

In the Christmas story, the wise men show us God's intent to honor the wonderful skills of curious mathematic minds that observe the heavens above. In that house, when those three humble and teachable scientists drew around Christ, they immediately fell to worship Him. I believe this is God's way of showing us that although we attempt to understand the amazing intricacies of our world and everything beyond it that we can, we are just scratching the surface when it comes to His capabilities. God cannot be defined by man. The Creator is above His creation because He is the Source behind its existence.

Faith Is a Substance Measurable Only by God...for Now!

Just like the mind and the spirit coexist in a human being, so at the feet of Jesus that day, science and religion coexisted in the house of Joseph and Mary, and science bowed—because once you get a glimpse of Jesus, all your ideas about who God is cannot compare or compete.

Faith is a spiritual concept. Today, science has problems with faith because they are looking for something natural—but faith is a spiritual concept and is called the substance of things hoped for and the evidence of things *not* seen, according to Hebrews 11:1. So, this is not something tangible or measurable, but it is something that exists as a "substance" created by God. It is beyond what science can prove because spiritual substances aren't natural—but that doesn't mean they aren't real.

Today, there are many people who do not believe in anything that cannot be proven in the ways that science can currently prove things. Yet science is always expanding and growing in capability, because people are always building upon the past and striving to know more. Today, they know more than they did yesterday—thank God, man is always growing and learning. Who knows? As a person of faith, I figure that one day, maybe, they just might catch up to God—they just may be able to find and measure the substance we call faith. I believe the more humble and teachable we are as people, the more open-minded we become; and it takes an open mind to learn and gain greater knowledge about whatever it is we are pursuing in life.

God does what He does regardless of a man's choice to believe Him or not—the divine doesn't stop and always is expanding no matter what we do. And the Magi are a good example that we can live both rationally and spiritually and find Jesus at the same time.

NEW LIGHTS DON'T
EXTINGUISH OLD TRUTHS

Just like it's a mistake to throw out faith if you also believe in science, it's also a mistake to throw away the past just because you are living in the present and goaling for the future. New lights don't have to extinguish old truths—there is so much that is profitable to learn from looking at the past. That's true whether you're reflecting on the Law of Moses, the Christmas story, or the past in your own life.

Where you are going in your life now doesn't make where you were before irrelevant. Is the past irrelevant? *No.* Is it profitable at times to look back and learn from what happened? *Yes.* We do a disservice to ourselves when we ignore history—whether it's biblical history, world history, or our own personal history.

We shouldn't throw away the Old Testament just because we've got the New Testament—the whole of it is our story, and we should enjoy both because we've got both! The Ten Commandments may be under the law, but are they still good rules to follow in life? Absolutely. This kind of "one side or the other side" mentality tends to set people up to fail because it sets people up to fight—and very little good is done in a state of strife.

We need both faith and works, grace and accountability to God. Grace doesn't mean we throw out our need for forgiveness. The whole of the Word is profitable for us. There are lessons in the Old Testament that matter so much, and we only lose when we disregard them. Proverbs alone is filled with everyday wisdom we can use!

Jesus explains the heart of matters and there is no greater Teacher than God Himself in the flesh. But every person in the Bible has something to teach us—they wouldn't be in the Word of God if they didn't. Even the most ancient of stories illustrate truths that are applicable in our modern times because the human nature has not changed. The Christmas story is layered with lessons. And the Holy Spirit will show you the ones you personally need for your future, if you just take time to honor the past and receive its good wisdom.

Chapter 10

Three Rich Gentiles Came to Worship and Give: Why Do We Fixate on the Manger's Hay?

The Magi followed what they could see in the natural, and they honored God by following the sign that He put in the night sky. We don't have to stare up at the sky or on the road as we drive along looking for signs because, as believers, our "sign" is the cross. Anything else is a cherry on top! Jesus was born to die— His purpose was to come, teach, and die to redeem us from sin, hell, death, and the grave. Death loses its sting in light of eternal life with God. We start to see this life as the vapor it really is—and we then start to enjoy our time a whole lot more.

It's the most wonderful time of the year because it's a time when we *pause*. The joys of Christmas are chockablock full with all the best things in life. Jesus! Family! Friends! Decking the halls and fa-la-la-

la-laaaaing are rooted in the reality that God loves people—and He is the greatest Giver. He gave us His only Son. Now, we give too!

We are not wandering like the unredeemed, looking only for signs. Since Jesus came and died and made a way for us to be close to the Father once again, we are led by *much* better lights.

THE MAGI FOLLOWED A SIGN, THE "STAR OF BETHLEHEM"— WE FOLLOW GOD'S WORD, WORKS, AND SPIRIT

God draws us near by His Word, His works, and His Spirit. We don't follow a star to get into the house of God. We follow the Word of God and obediently come home. We follow the works of God and stand amazed at His demonstrative love. We follow the Spirit of God and are led into peace, joy, and greater love for everyone around us, including ourselves.

Christmas has a feeling to it that can't be denied, and if there were one word to sum it up it would be love. Throughout life, there are many winding roads—we can go this way or that way, but God's road is always one that is marked by love.

God's Word is filled with a call to faith and love—and to do works that are marked by those two. Faith without corresponding action is just a bunch of words, and we are called to do a lot more than just talk! God calls us by His works when we read Jesus saying things like, *"He that believeth on Me, the works that I do shall he do also; and greater works than these shall he do; because I go unto My Father"* (John 14:12). God calls us by His Spirit when we read things like, *"Howbeit when He, the Spirit of truth, is come, He will guide you into all truth*" (John 16:13). You don't need guidance if you aren't going anywhere in life! God promises to guide us with His truth—but it's up to us to get up and go.

Sometimes, God will send you signs, but they are a blessing in addition to the way He intends us to grow and be guided. If the Word is the full meal, a sign is just an unexpected snack!

RICH GENTILES BRINGING THEIR **BEST**

The Magi show us by example that giving our best is a good idea. They were Gentiles, moved by natural phenomenon, and traveled very far to see the Christ child—and the whole way, they were carrying something they considered precious. Why? Because they wanted to give.

The wise men didn't bring the shabby, cast-off junk that they didn't want anymore. This wasn't a plastic bag full of used junk nobody wanted. This wasn't a sack full of the cans of vegetables they didn't like. The Magi didn't even start the journey before deciding that they were going to honor this person by bringing their *best*.

I like to say that if the Magi were from South Louisiana, they would have brought twelve sacks of crawfish, oysters, shrimp, and crabs! They would have brought pots of gumbo and bowls of rice. They would have had a fryer on the back of the camel and enough catfish to feed the whole town. Their wives would have probably sent them with twelve million desserts too. If the wise men were from Louisiana, that house would have been filled with more well-seasoned food than the house had room to hold!

There was nothing lack-oriented about the gifts of the Magi—they each brought what was best from their own countries. Today, when people read the Christmas story, they just love to focus on the lowly manger, as if this was Mary and Joseph's first choice or as if that's where the baby Jesus grew up. By the time the wise men found Jesus, the manger was long gone.

WHY DO WE KEEP JESUS IN THE MANGER? WHY DO WE FIXATE ON THE HAY?

Why do people want to fixate on the hay of the manger instead of the abundant gifts of gold, frankincense, and myrrh? Why do we focus on the manger instead of the house? I believe it's because people think that abundance and spirituality are like oil and water. Many think you can't have anything nice and be sincere spiritually because we've been taught for centuries that poverty is holy and sincerity must be marked by lack. People like thinking of the shepherds as poor. They like seeing Christ in the hay. Why? Because people often relate to lack, and they even want their God to be seen in some way as lacking.

This is why, I believe, so many people want to keep Jesus in the manger—it's simply because they can better relate. They can't seem to mix spirituality with abundance. A huge wall of *"no"* comes into their mind at the thought of it.

Now, I love that Jesus *began* in the manger—but He didn't *stay* in a manger. Still, the manger shows us that it doesn't really matter where we start; even if we start in the lowest place, God will make sure we finish well if we stick with Him. No matter where we come from, even if it's unplanned or undesirable, God is with us, love is all around us, and we aren't destined to stay in a low place if we are following God. That's just where we're starting!

Jesus went from sleeping in the hay to sitting on the throne in Heaven, and we are all destined to be seated with Him in high places one day. In the meantime, we get to pursue what He came to give us—which is life and life more abundantly. Jesus said that. We get to learn to see the pitfalls and the devil's devices—anything that kills, steals, or destroys isn't of God. Jesus said that.

Keeping Jesus in a manger isn't a wise thing people do; it's just a status-quo, lack-mentality, habitual thing people do. Especially at Christmas. We don't sing "Joy to the World" because lack came. We sing "Joy to the World" because the Answer to man's sin-sick heart problems came! Through reconnection with God by way of Jesus, we get the answer to all the problems of our own heart so that we can live more abundantly in every way—spiritually, physically, mentally, financially, and in our relationships with others, too. Everything good that pertains to life and godliness is abundance-oriented.

It's ridiculous how a poverty mindset can cause some people to walk around dripping with self-righteous hypocrisy—working for a living and dreaming of more, but despising money itself as the root of all evil. It's the *love of money* that is evil, the scripture tells us, and there are many people walking around loving money who don't have any. Greed is not good, but abundance through God is wonderful! It makes all the times of the year wonderful. The Magi had no problem with nice stuff, and in fact lugged their best gifts over a long and perilous journey just to give them—because they recognized the importance of what they deemed their "best."

DON'T LET ANYBODY TALK YOU OUT OF ABUNDANCE— THERE'S NO "JOY TO THE WORLD" FOR HUNGRY CHILDREN

I always find it interesting that the very people who hate abundance will sell their books against it for profit. The very preachers who use the pulpit to castigate anyone with a dream of having more sure will pass the plate at offering time and expect your best then.

If the Magi were poor, they'd have had nothing to give. And if God didn't want them blessing the holy family with great things, He wouldn't have sent them on their way with gold, frankincense, and myrrh.

The Church seems to want the shepherds poor. They seem to want people poor today too. They seem to think it's wonderful and holy. But Christmas is marked by giving and receiving because of those Magi—rich Gentiles with a desire to worship God.

Although Christmas is the most wonderful time of the year, we all know it's not joyful for everyone. There's no "Joy to the World" for hungry children. In fact, people all around the world are starving because of poverty and lack. The "there's not enough" mindset that fills people's hearts with misery and leads them into lack in all areas is epidemic. Countries that are filled with natural resources still have abject poverty running wild. Why? It's a lack mindset that believes there is "never enough" that keeps the world believing there isn't enough—and all sorts of evil seems to ricochet off of it.

God created this planet with everything we need to eat, live, and thrive, but it's a lack mindset that fosters hopelessness as quickly as it compels leaders to hoard for themselves at the expense of their own people. You can send food all over the world, but if the national and local officials don't care about their people, they'll let that food rot in the trucks—and they'll do it while hoarding the best things for themselves. A lack mindset destroys hope just as easily as it creates the desire to hoard up. People who know there will always be enough don't seem to be as greedy with what they've got—some might still be, but most aren't, because it's out of that feeling of lack that the desire to hoard comes.

Jesus came to bring life, and that more abundantly. The abundant mindset of God starts with hope for our own unburdening and faith in Jesus' ability to take it through His own sacrifice on the cross. When we unburden our sin onto Jesus and receive forgiveness, we are accepting not only His forgiveness but also His great and abundant love—and it's that love, shed abroad in our heart, that changes us.

A man who has found Christ cannot stand by while a truck full of good food intended for the poor rots. A woman who has found Christ can't turn her eyes away from need and feel good about it. A teenager who has found Christ cannot turn the other way when the Holy Spirit prompts her to help someone, to give to someone. An abundant-minded believer, no matter where they live or how they were raised, becomes marked by a generous spirit. Christmas is flowing with this kind of spirit because it's a holiday founded on the love of God. I believe believers become distribution houses of goodness—not just words, but works—when they choose to accept that with God, there is not "just enough" but "more than enough" for every single good work.

If the Church preaches that the desire for abundance is somehow wrong, I believe we are literally harming society. The hope, faith, and love we preach should be founded on Jesus, the One Who came, redeemed us, and conquered the curse of Eden and gave us the victory, too. It's in a real and authentic relationship with Jesus that people realize that there is *more* than enough available in the world and available in God—for us, for our families, and for the whole world.

Society benefits from hope, faith, love, and an abundant mentality. Society benefits when the Church learns from the Magi and starts valuing both worship of God and gifts of abundance—because only people who have something to give *can* give. Giving makes the world go round! And through the Magi, God shows us that our best gifts are what we should always aim to give—without fear that there won't be enough for us after we give it.

WHAT ARE YOU GIVING JESUS?

The wise men came prepared with a gift to meet Jesus—what is your gift? It can be physical, spiritual, or financial, but your greatest gift is your heart. After that, you can go through life as if it's Christmas every day, giving to others in honor of God's gift to you in Christ. It's about your intention to give your best.

It feels wonderful to give "as unto the Lord." There is an openness to a mindset of giving that is very pure in nature. As believers, we should start to see everything we are doing as a type of giving. Every good thought we have toward someone, every good word or good deed, we should start seeing it as a gift we give to God. That's how giving becomes our lifestyle and becomes just part of who we are and not just what we do. That's how it becomes linked to worship.

When we give to others as unto the Lord, it's as if we are laying gold, frankincense, and myrrh at the feet of Jesus in Joseph and Mary's house! And each gift becomes a seed we sow, which comes back to us so that we can give more. The cycle of giving and receiving is a wonderful thing!

Chapter 11

The Simple Faith, Undoubting Obedience, and Deep, Loving Reverence of the Magi

Sometimes simple faith gets the best results. The Magi had simple faith, undoubting obedience, and a deep, loving reverence for whoever would fulfill the prophecy and be king—and yet they were Gentiles. They just said, "Well, the prophecy must be true, the skies are telling us that much…we've got to go and worship the king!" You see, they just had simple faith and started going, prepared to meet a king with the best gifts they had to offer.

In the wise men, we learn that simple faith often is what brings you to the feet of Christ. Simple faith always gets the best results. It's the people who are mulling over whether what God said was true or not who end up in a tiny room somewhere, confused, when they should be sitting at the feet of Jesus.

I find it astounding that while Jesus was a Jew and was promised to the Jews, it was the Gentiles who first sought Him out. You know, the Magi couldn't have been the only ones seeing that star of Bethlehem. Plenty of people of faith likely saw that celestial phenomenon, too. Yet only the ones with simple faith followed it.

There are people who love to argue in the world. There are people who go to church, read the Word, listen to every message they can get their hands on—but still lack simple faith. They'd rather play with the words than follow the Word. It's a hobby to them, and the more antagonistic they can be, the better. The Magi's simple faith inspires me.

That no one followed the wise men as they followed the star astounds me, too. I think, hey, I'd kind of wonder what three guys from other countries were doing in my town and why they were following the crazy star in the sky. You know they had to talk to people along the way. Yet no one followed.

The Church is a lot like that—no matter what is said, some people just aren't following. You could say, "Jesus just came!" They'd say, "Can we watch Him from home? When's the rebroadcast?"

So many go to church out of sheer obligation—and even though the discipline itself of putting God first is important, I think God wants us to have our heart in it when we celebrate Him together at church. I don't think He'd want us griping about coming into His house. If you griped about coming to mine, I'd probably tell you to stay home! God isn't that way; He's merciful and open-armed, but you get the point.

At Christmas, a lot of people end up in church who don't want to be there. When I was young, I was at midnight mass drunk as a skunk…like so many other people! We had no clue what they said, because we couldn't remember the next morning—but we went, and that was all that was important. That is surely not giving our best to God!

YOU WILL NOT STAY IN DARKNESS WHEN YOU SEEK THE LIGHT IN FAITH

Melchior, Casper, and Balthazar may not have known all the scriptures but they knew enough to make their way to Jesus. You don't have to know everything to find the One Who made everything. All you need is simple faith to start moving in the direction of God.

No matter how much you are walking around in darkness, you can't stay in the darkness when you are seeking the Light of God. Jesus will pull you out of darkness and into His marvelous light—and He won't do it by telling you how horrible you are for being in the dark in the first place.

Light doesn't argue or even mess with the dark—it just obliterates it. Darkness literally cannot exist in a light place, but light can exist in a dark place. There are flashlights that beam light, but there aren't ones that beam darkness. It's impossible. Jesus is the Light of the world and when we go to Him for forgiveness, any darkness we've got is obliterated—it can't stay in His forgiving presence; it simply cannot. So, we don't have to talk about our dark past all day long. We get to let it go. He is more interested in pouring out His love on us than anything. Our faults and sins can't even compete with the Light of the World's capacity to forgive and scatter darkness like it never even existed.

When the wise men found Jesus, they fell on their faces to worship Him because that's what happens when people of simple faith, undoubting obedience, and a deep, loving reverence meet

God in the flesh. There is no earthly king who compares to the King of Kings, and we will all have that experience one day when we cannot stand before Him because our heart naturally wants to bow at the glory and love of God. Jesus was God here on the earth—God with skin so that the glory was contained enough not to blow everybody away.

IF JESUS HATED NICE THINGS, THE WISE MEN'S GIFTS WOULD HAVE BEEN REJECTED

Gold, frankincense, and myrrh were precious things and appropriate gifts for kings—that's what the wise men thought, and so that's what the wise men brought. Nobody seems to mind if kings have nice things. Riches, wealth, and the best of whatever they choose to enjoy—it's no big deal to people if kings have the best. Why is it such a big deal in the Church if God's people have the best? Did not God call us kings and priests under Him?

Sometimes we need to look at Who we belong to—and ask ourselves if God gave us this beautiful planet, teeming with life and life more abundantly, why do we sell ourselves so short and expect so little? If greater is He that is in us than he that is in the world, why are we so comfortable with the world having nice things but not very comfortable with God's children having nice things?

If Jesus gave us principles like faith to use for the *things* we want to receive or remove in life—revolutionary ways of thinking, talking, and acting in accordance with God's Word—why do some people fight "the faith message" so much? Do we really think that God is worried about His children having the "gold, frankincense, and myrrh" of our day? God isn't living in poverty—and when He made man, He didn't create him to enjoy poverty. Eden was lush, plentiful, and teaming with abundant life. Nothing changed until Satan came into the picture and deceived man into giving up God's best.

Jesus said that I can talk to the mountainous problems in life, tell them to be removed and cast into the sea, and if I don't doubt but believe what I say, well, I'll have "whatsoever" I say (Mark 11:23). What part of "whatsoever" has a limit on it?

Faith moves (with the mind and mouth) what the eyes think is a fixed reality. Faith changes reality. People change what they see with what they believe and what they say across the world. I am always hearing testimonies of people who say God healed them, delivered them, and gave them favor or financial blessings. It's part of my everyday life to hear testimonies from people who have been changed by their faith in God's Word. I've seen it so many times in my own life; nobody will ever be able to tell me that it's not true—because the evidence of my unseen faith has created so much of what I see in my life today. My life's work has been and continues to be dedicated to helping people find God so that they can move those mountains in their life and start living the abundant life God created His children to live.

We live in a sin-sick world that calls what is bad good and what is good bad—that is how the Bible says it will be in the last days, and I believe we are in those "last days." Being a wealthy believer means that you can finance the Gospel in a greater way, and that means you can help to introduce more people to Jesus. I believe Satan has attacked the abundance message deliberately to stop the spread of good—because the more people are truly changed by God's love, the better society gets...and that's just not good for business in Satan's eyes.

He wants people to remain in the darkness. He wants to keep the world spinning in distraction, malice, hatred, immorality—lust and desire for what cannot ever really fulfill the human heart. All he has is the flesh to work with, so that's what he tempts. He has convinced the Church that it should be poor, because a poor church and a struggling people can't affect the world very much. He's very happy for us to be mentally stuck on the hay! He'd like us to think only kings can have the gold, the frankincense, and the myrrh of life. His goal is to keep us down, quiet, and too shameful to even speak the name of Jesus.

Well, if you know my ministry, you know that I don't care what the devil wants—I will be blessed in the city, blessed in the field, blessed coming in, and blessed going out. If God said I could have something, then I can have it. Blessed, rich, healthy, walking in the power of my own faith in God—I don't shrink back in shame for the blessings of God on my life any more than I shrink back when it comes to talking about God or His Word.

"They" can call me arrogant, cocky, or whatever—I know that I'm just confident in what I believe because I take God's Word over their word, and I refuse to make an excuse for the blessings of God on my life. Before I was saved, I was loud for the devil. I'd get drunk and fall down, smoke dope, and pop pills. I took trips and never left my house. I didn't care what anybody thought of me.

Now that I am born again, why should I hold back from speaking about God? Why should I be quiet about who I am now? I serve the Lord, and I've got a lot to say! He's helped me and I never want to go back to living in darkness. So, I'll pray at the restaurants, I'll pray in the mall, and I'll pray or talk about God wherever I want to— because I can, and because it's good! I serve a living God, not a dead religion. If the wise men had the guts to tell a lying devil from hell like Herod that the Jews had a new king, then I sure can talk about Jesus in my own life, too.

Chapter 12

Nothing Could Stop the Magi, Don't Let Anything Stop You

Another lesson to be learned from the Magi is this: The journey may have been hard, but they didn't shrink from making it—nothing could stop the Magi from following God's guiding light, and nothing should stop you from following it either.

The Magi journeyed about 1,500 miles to get to Jesus—and that was a risky endeavor because many of those miles were dangerous. Bandits were known to steal from foreigners passing through, and these men were rich. They were carrying those expensive gifts, and they knew it. They just wanted to meet Christ bad enough to go forward in their plan anyway—and besides, they saw that light in the sky. They knew it was something they had to do. You see, for the Magi, the reward of meeting Christ was worth the risk of those who might try to take advantage of their goodness along the way.

If God is drawing you somewhere, of course you want the journey to be easy—who doesn't want easy? But most of the places God calls us to or the things in life He calls us to do require a degree of bravery and risk—it's called faith! You just have to know He's guiding you. You just have to keep following the light He's shining on your path. Like the Magi, you just have to get to the place in your mind where nothing is going to stop you from getting where you want to go.

You can't be afraid of what people might say or do to you when you are pointed in a direction that you know God is leading you to go. If He's drawing you, if He's shining His light on your path, you have to go—fear can't stop you. You might feel it rise up, but don't let it stop you from moving forward.

It's in your best interests to go, even if the road looks rocky ahead and even if you know the sidewalk is filled with people who would like nothing better than to stop you. Remember that God is with you always, and that means there is more with you than there is with them. Being led by the Lord changes everything, and He guides us by His Spirit like He guided the Magi with the star of Bethlehem.

God will make sure we get to where we need to be in life if we follow Him—and remember, He's not above giving last-minute instructions! Like the dream He gave the wise men to go back home another way, God is known to intervene to get us to safety.

Who knows what Herod would have done had they gone back? Nervous kings do unpredictable things. God brought them safely to their destination and gave them instruction that sent them back home safely, too.

I can't tell you how many times the Holy Spirit has prompted me not to go this way or that way, not to get on a certain plane or to stay behind. Sometimes I've been able to see why and other times I haven't, but I've just come to a point in my faith that I trust the promptings of God. He looked out for the wise men; He is looking out for me—and I promise, if you follow His Spirit, He'll look out for you, too!

THE MAGI WERE SEARCHING FOR LIVING BREAD

Bethlehem means "house of bread." Jesus is often called "living bread." And I can tell you that when the wise men were on the hunt for the king of the Jews, they sure weren't interested in finding stale bread!

One of the lessons that comes up for me when I think about the references to bread is that we, the Church, are supposed to be walking in life—and yet so many people want nothing to do with church because when they think about Christians, they get a bad taste in their mouth. Why? How many of us are really *living*?

Maybe the reason people don't care for church is because they know that all they'll get if they go is a message of stale bread. We've made Jesus stale when He was, is, and is always going to be a force of light and life. There's nothing stale about Jesus.

Fresh bread is wonderful—but you can use stale bread like a hammer to get a nail in the wall! Fresh fish is wonderful—old fish makes your nose hairs curl! Fresh flowers on the vine smell great—but if you cut them off and stick them in a vase by your sink, you'll be lucky to keep them a week before they start to decay and smell like the swamp.

God intends for His people to live this life with gusto—to enjoy it, to squeeze all the goodness out of this great gift, and to share with others the joys we have found in life. Jesus is the greatest joy I've ever found in my life, and it gives me pleasure to talk about Him with others. I don't have stale Christianity; I enjoy a fresh life of faith. Why? Because I found the Living Bread, and there's no way I want to live by some stale idea of God when I have the Source of everything that is new and good living inside of me.

Stir up the gift of God within you and refuse to eat stale crumbs when Living Bread is available. Following Christ is the best cure for the doldrums of life because He makes everything fresh and new. Following Jesus is definitely going to take you out of the comfort zone, just like it took the wise men out of their own comfort zones. Let's never get cozy nibbling on stale words or thinking stale thoughts when the Holy Spirit is right here with us, able to bring freshness into our lives. No matter how long you've been living or how long you've been saved, make a commitment to never go stale. Let's choose to never, ever get tired of feasting on the Living Bread!

THE OBJECT OF THE MAGI'S QUEST— WORSHIP!

Why do we go to church? Why do we serve God? What is the reason why we have chosen to include Christ in our lives? Is it only for us—for what we can receive from Him? Is it only for the principles that teach us how to "live our best life" now? Through their quest to find Christ, the Magi teach that maybe the best reason we can ever have for wanting to see Jesus is to worship.

We're such an independent people today that the concept of worship is often lost on us—but I believe that is simply because so many people do not know God for themselves. If all you see is flawed human beings, it's difficult to understand why we would worship anyone or anything at all. God is not human, though, and even Christ was only partly—a mix of God's Holy Spirit and Mary's womb, Jesus was worthy of worship.

Jesus was no earthly king. He was the King of Kings, and the object of the Magi's quest to find Him ended with them flat on their faces in worship. Again, these were not Jews. Rich Gentiles were the only ones who seemed to understand the power behind that small face staring back at them that day.

One day we will all see Jesus face to face, and on that day the toughest of men and hardest of hearts will do just what the wise men did—every knee will bow and every tongue will confess that Jesus is Lord. You see, when the Magi saw Him, they only saw His human form, but when we see Him next, we will see the true magnitude of His glory—and it will be so obvious to us that there is no better gift or tribute we can give Him than to humble ourselves before Him in sincere *worship*.

The scribes and Pharisees wouldn't have anything to do with Christ then. Today, we have Messianic Jews who honor Jesus as Lord, but most Jews then and now still don't have anything to do with Jesus. After all, how could a Messiah be born in a stable? Such a lowly place! A leader of the people should not start this way, they assumed—but the Magi didn't think this way.

As kings, you'd think they would have mentioned Jesus' lowly start or criticized visiting a house instead of a palace—but they did not. Jesus left Heaven to come here, and anything even a palace would have still paled in comparison to where He came from anyway, but still—the wise men didn't flinch when they walked into the house where Christ lay. They lowered themselves, bowed, and fell to their knees in worship.

Immediately, they brought out their best gifts—gold from India, frankincense from Persia, and myrrh from Arabia. They brought what their natural lands had and gave, as it was their custom and duty to give when approaching a king. I believe that when we approach our King, we should give too—we should give our best gift, which is our own heart. The best thing we can give to Jesus is ourselves, because, above all, that is what He wants.

So, why should we go to church? We should go to worship our King! We should give ourselves in this way. Do we have other things that we could be doing? Of course, we have other things we *could* do. Of course, we can watch a sermon or a service on television or on the web too. That's not the point. We don't assemble with people of like precious faith in order just to *get* something from God—we assemble as a congregation to *give* something to God!

We humble ourselves. We show Him we put Him first. We give Him the gift of ourselves when we gather together to worship His holy name. I'm not just talking about singing. Plenty of churches have great singers and good bands. That doesn't mean anything. Worship comes from the heart. The worst singers who have a heart to worship do better than the best of entertainers who don't care about Christ at all. Our focus is the important thing, and our focus must be on Christ.

What happens when we are given so much from God? We can't help but praise and worship Him and give—something in our heart simply wants to give back to God. This is how God made us. And we use that desire to give back to promote the works of God on the earth as well as to reach out and help those right beside us in life. God's Spirit rubs off on us when we get close to Him in worship—and that leads to a life better lived, because that leads to a life of giving.

THE WAY WE LIVE AND GIVE: IT THROWS A FLOODLIGHT ON OUR CHARACTER AND OUR CAPACITY TO LOVE

People ask me all the time, "You give a lot, don't you?" I tell them that I do—but because I've become known for it. My giving goes before me, so to speak.

Giving was one of the first things I began to do after I gave my life to Jesus—it just naturally seemed like the right thing to do. I didn't see it so much as a duty but as an honor. I don't have to give; I *get* to give! Today, I can say that I've given away more money than some will ever make in a lifetime. I'm addicted to giving, and God supports my habit. The more I give, the more it comes back to me, and because I just keep giving, the cycle continues.

I like giving into what I call "good soil" because I know the rate of return is so much higher—but even if it isn't exactly good soil, I still enjoy the act of giving itself. It blesses me to bless others.

I'm not ashamed to give publicly or privately. Some say I should never mention it, but I believe they are just misguided—the scripture about not letting your right hand know what your left hand is doing in giving is about giving to the poor. And if you haven't noticed, I never talk about that or try to move people emotionally to give to the poor.

It is totally contrary to the Word of God to parade the poor in front of everyone, even in order to raise money for them. It destroys a poor person's dignity when people broadcast what they're giving to them—it puts people in the position of savior, when there is only one Savior and His name is Jesus. So, when I give to the poor (and I suggest you do this too), I am careful to give quickly, kindly, and with as little attention garnered as possible. This is the left hand/right hand scriptural way, and the purpose again is to maintain a person's dignity when they are in such a low and impoverished state.

Giving in general, however, that is a different thing! We learn through the Magi that giving your best and doing it publicly is favorable to God—He would not have moved upon the wise men to give if He didn't approve of the idea. We also would have something in the scripture criticizing it if it was worthy of being criticized—but it's not. Giving is wonderful. It goes hand in hand with worship, and I believe it throws a floodlight for all to see on our character and our capacity to love.

Those who don't give aren't just stingy in that one area, they are usually stingy in every area of life—and so, if there is a problem with giving, there is usually a problem with fear that keeps the person from giving. Love gives and the perfect love of God casts out all fear—including the fear of "I don't have enough to give." I find that we always have something to give. It's not always about money. We need to see everything good that we do as a form of giving—as unto the Lord, and also just because we know that it is good for our heart and our future.

THE MAGI TEACH US TO SEEK

We can wait for people to find us, or we can make it our business to discover them. We shouldn't wait for others to bring up God. If God is a part of our lives, then we should bring Him into our conversations—to open the door for people to maybe find Him through us. You never know where people are in their hearts and minds. If we only stay superficial in speaking with people, if we are not authentic, and if we never talk about our faith, how can God use us to witness? What seeds of faith can we plant if we never touch the soil?

As a believer, I don't wait for people to ask me about God. I pepper all my conversations with "God talk" because it's who I am—it's not just about what I do. Sure, I'm a preacher, but that doesn't matter. Plenty of preachers don't bother talking about God very much outside of their own churches. I bring my salvation with me everywhere I go. I bring my love for God with me everywhere I go. How could I stay silent about the One Who has changed me so much? It's going to end up in conversations in some way or another.

The Magi teach us to be seekers—because you can't always wait for others to come to you, spiritually or any other way. We shouldn't just assume that we don't need to tell others about our faith because they already know. It's a great possibility that they don't know or don't know how much it means to you. We can't assume they'll be offended, because there is a great possibility they will never be offended. Unless you are hollering at somebody or cutting someone down and then trying to talk about Jesus (don't do this!), just being yourself and sharing from your own life is rarely going to offend someone. In fact, even scoffers sometimes end up coming around—I can't tell you how many letters I've gotten from people who begin with, "I used to hate all preachers…" Ha!

Open your heart, open your mouth, and just see for yourself how good it feels to share from your own heart. People tend to be a little softer, more loving, and more open to goodness in the earth at Christmas anyway. Let your light shine! Learn from the Magi and don't be afraid to go to others instead of waiting for them to come to you.

FIND YOURSELF IN ONE OF THE FOUR TYPES OF PEOPLE

Three Gentiles crossed the desert to meet the King of Kings long ago, but we don't have to do that today. You know, I've crossed that desert in a plane. I've flown over many deserts, many oceans and seas—I've been all around the world. The difference between the Magi and me and the Magi and you is that we aren't looking for Christ—we are now carriers of Christ on this earth. We're not looking for the Gospel; we're bringing the Gospel to the world.

As I see it, there were four types of people at the time of Christ's birth: 1) the Magi—they were the seekers of truth; 2) the scribes and Pharisees—they were those who were resting in the letter of the truth; 3) King Herod and all of Jerusalem—they were the ones alarmed by the truth; and 4) Joseph and Mary—they were the affectionate guardians of the truth.

We still have these four types of people on the earth today, and at Christmas it's more evident just who is who. Can you find yourself in one of these four types? I hope you find yourself in the Magi— always seeking more of Christ, always quick to worship, and a person known for giving their best to God and to others. I also hope you find yourself in Joseph and Mary too—always remaining steadfast in your faith, and an affectionate guardian of the truth.

Mary was always controversial, you know. Let's take a look now at Mary—the one some love so very much and others love so very little, and yet still no one can deny…the only woman in the whole world whom God chose to mother His Son.

Mary, Mother of Jesus

THE FAVORED, THE BLESSED, THE ONE GOD CHOSE TO RAISE HIS ONLY SON, JESUS

Chapter 13

Mary, the Controversial

Nobody seems to appreciate Mary like the Catholics. When I was born, my mother and father were Catholic just like nearly everybody else in South Louisiana where I grew up. We weren't what you call "good Catholics" though—we went to mass on Christmas and Easter like the rest of the heathens who weren't really interested in changing. Still, we knew enough to know that Mary was critically important to the faith, and if we wanted anything at all from God, we might want to check with her first. "Jesus can't tell His mother 'no,' so pray to Mary," they told us. We believed them but didn't pray much anyway. They could have told us to pray to a rock and I think we would have nodded…to keep from falling asleep.

My dad had a miraculous recovery from an accident on an oil rig that blinded him, and that changed everything. Crying up a storm in a locked bedroom with my mother banging at the door, Daddy was in hysterics. He was a manual laborer and needed his eyes to work. He didn't know what he was going to do. That night, seeing nothing but darkness no matter what he did, Daddy made a promise to God in the middle of his brokenness: "God, if You heal my eyes, I promise I'll raise my kids to know You!" My dad kept hack-crying and kept praying all night long until his body just gave in to sleep. Meanwhile, God heard his prayer, and in the morning Daddy could see.

That was it for Mary. We cancelled our plans for the next Easter and Christmas with the Catholics, and from that point on we hooked up with the Protestants. Mama and Daddy dragged my brother Wayne and me from church to church, with my dad searching for one Protestant denomination that he thought had it right. Going from Catholic to Baptist is a culture shock, just like going from Lutheran to Church of Christ, to Church of God, to Assembly of God…to wherever. Now, our family was poor and full of dysfunction. Nobody knew God in a real way yet or how to apply any of the teachings outside of the Ten Commandments, and even some of those were fuzzy—but that didn't matter because it seemed like all Daddy cared about was that we were in church every time the door was open.

So, my family kept a lot of their dysfunctional thinking, talking, and acting. It wasn't until we landed in the Pentecostal Holiness faith that Daddy really felt settled—it was as strict a religion as there was, and I guess to Daddy that was worth his eyesight! I think he thought we had to have it hard to please God, and I think he was truly searching for pure faith. Mary, who might have had a slight nod here and there in a sermon during Christmas at every other church we went to, got the shaft down at the Pentecostal Holiness church. So, I saw Mary go from being fully adored as a young child to fully ignored and a whole lot worse as an older child.

In some churches, what you are "against" is far more important than what you are "for"—and in our town, in our church, that was definitely the case! Everything was a sin and everybody in our church hated you talking about Mary. You'd swear all the oxygen would be sucked out the room with the gasps if you brought the words "Catholic" and "Mary" up in the same sentence.

When I was young, everybody in that church seemed to think that since the Catholics went too far with worshipping Mary, they should bring the balance by either ignoring Mary altogether or viciously attacking the idea that her name should be spoken in the first place! I guess you could say that they were in league with the devil on that one. Because while nobody in our church seemed to put any stock or any faith in Mary, God sure did—and He sent an angel to tell her so right to her face.

Now, as you already know, this book is about the uncommon lessons I found as I read through the Christmas story, not the obvious ones. So here are a few interesting things I learned about Mary and God's promise to redeem mankind.

GOD ALWAYS KEEPS HIS PROMISES

Satan didn't believe in Mary very much. He didn't really know if Jesus was "the One" God had talked about in the Garden of Eden all those years back. Since the fall of mankind, Satan and the rest of the fallen had spent quite a few years looking for the One whom God said would come and "crush his head" as he "bruised His heel."

He had made sure Abel was killed quickly because, well, he was the "good one" of the two and Satan figured, who knows? He might be the one. Abel wasn't the one. So Satan spent a lot of time looking at men and women being born, living, and dying—and killing any prophet he could get his hands on. His deceiving tactics continue.

His stealing, killing, and destroying job continues as well. Time just keeps marching on.

So by the time Mary comes along, Satan isn't really as sharp as he once was. He's been spiritually dead for so long by then that his capacity to notice the real thing is fading. Time has a funny way of making everyone, even fallen angels, forget that God *always* keeps His promises.

MARY'S HUMILITY AND FAITH WERE NOTICED: SHE EMBODIED PASSIONATE OBEDIENCE AND TRUE PURITY OF HEART

When we think of "the Virgin Mary," we often think of how she's always portrayed—meek and mild-mannered. But just because one is innocent and a virgin doesn't mean that they are weak or mild.

Have you seen very many little girls in your life? All of them virgins, yet all of them quite different. Virginity itself is not a personality or character trait, and yet for Mary, throughout the ages, virginity itself has become a defining factor in how we think of her and understand her character.

However, to me, Mary's character is marked by humility, faith, passionate obedience, and purity of heart. When I look at the Christmas story and when I imagine Mary, I see a passionate young woman of faith—a strong woman in a pure state. She had an uncommon trait of blunt faith in God—a quickness to move on what God said, without second-guessing Him through reasoning, doubt, or worry about her future.

Mary was innocent in her body when the angel Gabriel came, but it seems she was wise beyond her years in faith before he ever showed up. God chose her for a reason—and I believe it was because she had what it took not only to hear and receive the message from God, but also to carry the divine secret, raise Jesus correctly, and live the life necessary for her role as the mother of God's only Son.

Let's look at the scriptures in Luke 1:26-45 together now and I'll interject some thoughts as we go along to share a few of the unusual things I noticed in looking at this old, familiar text.

MARY CAME LAST TO MEN OF HER TIME, BUT NOT TO GOD

"And in the sixth month the angel Gabriel was sent from God unto a city of Galilee, named Nazareth, To a virgin espoused to a man whose name was Joseph, of the house of David; and the virgin's name was Mary" (verses 26-27). Did you notice that Mary's name is mentioned last? The angel, Joseph, his lineage, and even the status of her sexuality are all listed before we even read her name—the writer of Luke was a man of his time, and in that day men did not esteem women too highly.

If you think it's a man's world today (and it is in many ways), it is still nothing by comparison to what it was back then. Men in that time didn't think of women as even close to equals. Most women took a back seat even to their male children. Nothing could further ruin a woman's future faster than *not* being a virgin when she was supposed to be.

Mary's defining factor is her sexual status in the eyes of most of the men of her time, and as I said earlier, it's still a defining factor when we think about her character today—and although God wanted to use a virgin, he sees Mary as much more than just that.

MARY IS GREETED WITH
IMMEDIATE **APPROVAL**

"And the angel came in unto her, and said, Hail, thou that art highly favoured, the Lord is with thee: blessed art thou among women" (verse 28). Notice that the messenger of God did *not* bring up Joseph, his lineage, or Mary's sexual status first. The first thing the angel says on God's behalf is "hail"—and this is like saluting someone or cheering them on, like greeting someone with immediate approval. In that one word, the angel let her know that God wanted her to know, "Mary, I approve of *you*."

If you think God is in a constant state of disapproval that is just not true—He sent Jesus to show us His love, to redeem us from the curse of sin and death, and to give eternal life to all who simply believe on Jesus. God is not constantly disappointed with you. He's in a constant state of love for you.

You see, God knows who we all are inside at our very core. He sees the end from the beginning and knows all the "whys" people do this or that—He knows the physical DNA side, the soulish side, and the spiritual side of all of us. He may not approve of everything we do, but He definitely and at all times approves of who we *are*.

HIGH LEVEL FAVOR, DIVINE CONNECTION,
BLESSING IN WOMANHOOD:
THE FEMININE HEART IS VALUABLE TO GOD

So, when the angel came and said, *"Hail, thou that art highly favoured, the Lord is with thee: blessed art thou among women,"* he was speaking three things over Mary: 1) high level favor; 2) divine connection; and 3) blessing in womanhood.

Notice that the favor that rested upon Mary was mentioned even before she received the birth announcement. The connection she had with God is also acknowledged before she ever is told she will carry God's Son. And the fact that she is singled out as blessed among women—that too is spoken before any mention of what will soon change her whole life. She is honored in her womanhood, which is such an uncommon thing to say if you think about it.

Today, people often want to dismiss the feminine, as if just talking about it brings some kind of "less than" connotation—but God doesn't think of women as second-class citizens. To Him, they are valued for the unique creation that they are. They are not less important or more important than men, but equally important and wonderful in God's eyes, with differing characteristics of God's heart. To be blessed among women is to be singled out for the purpose of praise within the context of womanhood, something that God loves and values. The angel was literally praising Mary, which means that God was giving Mary praise too.

God values both men and women, and the feminine heart is very valuable to God regardless of the culture females are living within. God often values different things than what our cultures value, because He is not motivated by mankind's lacking viewpoints. He sees the whole picture, including the feminine and masculine natures of people. God loves praising His children for who they are at their core—He looks at the heart and sees potential for amazing growth in Him.

When God looked at Mary, He found just the kind of feminine heart He was looking for to raise His only Son—open, faithful, quick to believe, and capable of holding what is dear deep inside her own heart. Mary is not the kind of woman who needs a lot of outside support, even at a very young age. But she does need a few people, and God makes sure she has those few. What Mary says next shows how little time she spends thinking about herself and, possibly, how little she hears good words about herself in her everyday life.

MARY WAS TROUBLED BY GOD'S GOOD WORDS ABOUT HER

"And when she saw him, she was troubled at his saying, and cast in her mind what manner of salutation this should be" (verse 29). Mary is shocked—but not that a huge angel of God is staring her in the face, and not that he is talking directly to her, but she is shocked *"at his saying."* Mary is a listener; she is not an arguing type of woman. While some would have hit the dirt and would have been shaking in their shoes, Mary intently listened to the words about her. She's taking it in, not just reacting.

Like we all are, Mary is a product of her own time and environment. She lives in a man's world. She's not only humbled by the kind words of praise, though, she is troubled—troubled by good words. Mary is uncomfortable with compliments. Why? Perhaps because she lives in an era when she most likely hears so few good words about herself.

How many women walk the earth today not hearing good things about their character? Many, I imagine. How many never hear words of praise about the goodness that they carry in their heart? Again, I imagine many. Does it mean it isn't there? Of course not. It just means no one is speaking it directly—although they should.

I want you to notice that God has no problem complimenting the character of a woman—He created women and loves them. While the rest of the world primarily looks on the outward appearance of women and judges them that way, God always looks at the heart because that is where you find out what a woman is really made of.

Beauty is one thing, but character is another. So, it's not the outfit or the shoes that make the woman, although I believe a woman should be able to wear great things that make her feel good. And it's not the makeup or what the world tries to sell a woman that makes a woman. The most valuable thing to God about a woman is the heart and soul of the woman herself, and that is what God values most in all women, including Mary.

To be greeted so directly by an angel sent from God with those kinds of wonderful words takes Mary aback. When she thinks, "What manner of salutation should this be?" it's because she's puzzled by such good words. Mary is likely the kind of girl who prizes what she does and not who she is—and yet in her actions up until that point, she is developing the character that God needs to parent His Son.

MARY WASN'T CHOSEN BECAUSE SHE WAS PERFECT

"And the angel said unto her, Fear not, Mary: for thou hast found favour with God" (verse 30). Again, favor! The angel is not repeating himself; he's letting Mary know that she is not only "highly favored" but she has also "found favor with God"—which means she's doubly favored! What is favor? It is *unmerited* grace. It's *unmerited* kindness. It's like when a superior bends down in kindness to an inferior to help them.

In other words, Mary might have been actively doing good deeds during her life up until then, but God didn't choose her because she was a perfect woman. God chose her because she had the perfect heart for the position, and He considered her the best choice among women in her time.

How many women go through life thinking God can't possibly love them or use them for something great because they aren't perfect? God is not seeking perfection. He's not looking for perfect women; He's looking for willing hearts. Nobody is perfect but Jesus—not even the Virgin Mary. Yet she had characteristics we can learn from, and one is just knowing the importance of cultivating a godly and loving heart. Who doesn't want to be doubly favored by God? We all do!

MARY IS NOT ONLY GOOD-HEARTED, BUT PRACTICALLY-MINDED

The angel continues, *"And, behold, thou shalt conceive in thy womb, and bring forth a Son, and shalt call His name JESUS. He shall be great, and shall be called the Son of the Highest: and the Lord God shall give unto Him the throne of His father David: And He shall reign over the house of Jacob for ever; and of His kingdom there shall be no end"* (verses 31-33).

The kingdom of Jesus will never end. That's not a shot against other religions—but Jesus was Godsent, and His kingdom is not manmade. When Mary was given this birth announcement in Luke 1:31-33, she was told about her son's future. Jesus would be great, others would call Him the "Son of the Highest," and God would give Him the throne of His forefather David, where He'd reign over the house of Jacob forever—having a kingdom that would never end. David was not just an earthly king; he was a king in the people's hearts. He was loved and continued to be loved to that day, even though his reign had long ended. The people felt like they were David's people. Mary was told that her son, on the other hand, would have a kingdom where there really was no end.

Mary had a question: *"Then Mary said unto the angel, How shall this be, seeing I know not a man?"* (verse 34). Notice she doesn't doubt; she asks for an answer—she is pondering but not doubting. Mary is not only good-hearted but also practically-minded. She is a virgin. She doesn't deny that it will happen as the angel said; she asks *how* it will happen. God has no problem with this in people. Pondering is different from doubting. Faith and questioning can coexist. But know that God sees right down into our heart and He knows whether our questioning is curiosity or just plain doubt. Mary has curiosity but immediate faith; God sees and knows this—she just wonders how she, as a virgin, will conceive.

"And the angel answered and said unto her, The Holy Ghost shall come upon thee, and the power of the Highest shall overshadow thee: therefore also that holy thing which shall be born of thee shall be called the Son of God" (verse 35). So, God's messenger answers her—she is going to experience a miraculous physical insemination by way of the Holy Spirit. It's going to be a holy thing, not a fleshy thing. And out of God's miracle, she will have a son who will be called the Son of God. I believe had God told her to marry Joseph quickly and have a baby with him, she would have done that with just as much quick obedience—because what mattered to Mary was God's will, and if God asked her for something, she had the kind of character to step up to the plate and do it, no matter the cost.

Through the words God's messenger delivers, Mary finds out her son will be royal, holy, a beloved people's king, and his kingdom will last forever. She also knows she will receive the seed of Jesus into her womb without the aid of a man, which although she knows is a total impossibility naturally, she accepts as possible because she believes God. If that's what God said, then that's what will be—this is how Mary acts. Talk about faith!

You could call this a crisis moment in a way. And I believe that how you react in a crisis is determined by the habitual conduct of your past. Apparently, Mary had a habit of trusting God. She understood immediately when she saw that angel that God was talking, and if He were talking, she would listen. This is *very* strong faith at work—a faith that is as uncommon today as it was over two thousand years ago.

Chapter 14

A Divine Support System:
The Sacred Bond of
Two Women and Two Babies

ometimes we are in situations where we really do need someone
physically by our side who understands what we are going
through and will simply be with us as a support. Mary will not
have very many people like this in her life, but God makes sure she
has one amazing woman who knows exactly what it means to birth
something impossible.

God knew the time Mary lived in. He knew that few would
believe that she could conceive from the Holy Spirit as a virgin. So,
God let Mary know that He has given her a built-in support system
in Elisabeth, who is also experiencing her own "miracle" baby. *"And,
behold, thy cousin Elisabeth, she hath also conceived a son in her old age:
and this is the sixth month with her, who was called barren. For with
God nothing shall be impossible"* (verses 36-37).

John the Baptist's mother is already pregnant, but not by the Holy Spirit. Elisabeth is the older, barren woman now carrying Zacharias' baby—and yet the angel makes sure to let Mary know that this too is an impossibility made possible by God. In other words, "Mary, you're going to need a friend, and I've put one in your life who understands that God can do anything—she's going to have faith in God, believe what you say, and rejoice with you because she too knows exactly what it's like to have God touch your body and produce a miracle baby."

Women don't just need men in life, they need other women too. Women make the world go round. In my family, when my mother died, everything changed—because women change everything. Of course they can do anything out in the world, but to the people in their own house and in their own family, they are the bedrock of "home." Daddy can be gone for a week and everybody may feel it, but not in the same way as when a good mama is gone for a week. It's like the whole place starts falling apart!

Nothing is impossible with God, and God knows that sometimes you need a friend or a relative in your life to lean on and enjoy being with who can relate to whatever it is you're going through. Elisabeth is Mary's support system—and she's carrying Jesus' cousin in her womb who will also be a big support to Jesus.

I love how Mary responds. It is so simple. There is no doubt. There is only pure acceptance of God's message to her: *"And Mary said,* **Behold the handmaid of the Lord; be it unto me according to thy word.** *And the angel departed from her"* (verse 38). It's like Mary is saying, "Look at me, Angel—I want you to see me and see that I am a servant of God. Whatever He wants, I accept and will do. Let it happen, just as you said, Angel! I will serve God in any way that He needs."

That kind of immediate acceptance of such a huge event—one that will take her entire life in a different direction than if she had just lived a normal life—shows uncommon obedience and strong character. This woman had simple and pure faith, but she also wanted things to happen quickly! She didn't ponder about what it would mean for her to accept the role of Jesus' mother. She didn't argue about the name. She didn't say, "Let me ask Joseph what he thinks." No, Mary put God above everything—including her husband-to-be and herself. In that time, a husband's role was like king over his wife. Mary was young, in that environment, and still set all of that aside for God.

Think about what saying yes to God meant! It's as if she said, "I'll carry a baby that will make everybody think I'm not a virtuous woman, God. I'll be talked about badly behind my back and possibly harmed for this, God, but I'll do it. The man I love who has said he will marry me will likely not understand, but I'll put You even before him. He may leave me, I may end up in shame, and I may end up forever alone...but I want what You say, God, no matter what happens to me."

You can never forget that this is the Middle East over 2,000 years ago. This was *not* a time of equality for women at all—and yet Mary acted as if none of that mattered. God mattered to Mary. He called upon her and she was quick to say, "OK, God, whatever You want, I'll do it. I'm ready. Go!" This is not a meek and mild-mannered girl. This is a bold, young woman with character and faith like few others. There is a reason why God chose her among all the other women!

DIVINE CONNECTIONS FROM THE <u>WOMB</u>

Now, this is a kick in the head! God does some amazing things and this is one unusual event. Nobody talks about the fact that when

Mary met Elisabeth and they were both pregnant, Jesus, Who was one part of the Trinity of the Godhead, literally met and conversed with John the Baptist in the *womb*. That's right. Jesus met John in the womb through the miracle of baptism in the Holy Spirit.

*"And Mary arose in those days, and went into the hill country with haste, into a city of Juda; And entered into the house of Zacharias, and saluted Elisabeth. And it came to pass, that, when Elisabeth heard the salutation of Mary, the babe **leaped in her womb**; and Elisabeth was **filled with the Holy Ghost**"* (verses 39-41).

So God is talking to John—He's filling John with the Holy Spirit, which is like talking to both God and Jesus Christ at once. The Holy Trinity in action in the womb! They are meeting in the womb, and John is jumping in there having a Holy Ghost moment. He's speaking tongues in the womb. Who is he talking to? God, the Holy Spirit of God, and the spirit of Jesus—they are one in the same. This is how John meets Jesus for the first time. It was a divine connection from the womb.

Elisabeth was affected by this event. She felt that baptism happening in John—and it caused not only a physical leaping of his little body within her own, but a spiritual awakening in her as a mother as well. Elisabeth immediately knows what's happening with Mary and begins to prophecy it loudly: *"And she spake out with a loud voice, and said, Blessed art thou among women, and blessed is the fruit of thy womb"* (verse 42). Notice that Mary is called blessed again "among women" and her seed is called blessed too. There is a celebration of womanhood going on here between these women, as well as an acknowledgement of what God is doing in them both.

Elisabeth immediately knows Mary is carrying God in flesh form—and do you know the reason she suddenly just knows this?

It's because the Holy Spirit didn't just fill John, the Holy Spirit ran through the body and spirit of Elisabeth too, and she's so blown away by what is happening that she says this: *"And whence is this to me, that the mother of my Lord should come to me? For, lo, as soon as the voice of thy salutation sounded in mine ears, the babe leaped in my womb for joy. And blessed is she that believed: for there shall be a performance of those things which were told her from the Lord"* (verses 43-45).

In other words, Elisabeth is humbled and confirms for Mary that she has indeed heard from God. Elisabeth tells Mary, under the influence of the Holy Spirit, that everything said to her by the Lord will be performed. So, we have a divine connection being made between Jesus and John, and Mary and Elisabeth, and a confirmation of the angel's words. It is flat amazing.

From this point, Mary begins to sing from her heart in verses 46-55. She is using the words of her own mouth to now confirm what's happening to her—she's singing in praise but she's also confirming what she's heard again, reaffirming with her own heart and mouth that what God said will be done. Mary is on fire with inspiration that God recognized, blessed, and favored someone so seemingly "lowly" as herself. Mary knows that Heaven is a far cry from the state of affairs in her own country. She knows God in Heaven has honored her and she is more than just grateful.

What Mary doesn't realize, because she is a product of her time, is that God never thought of her as lowly at all. She was a queen of sorts in His eyes—a virgin in body, but a powerhouse in spirit. Young in body, but wise at heart. "Lowly" is just a human thought because God said He made man just a little "lower than Elohim"—in other words, God considered His creation *high* and not low. Just as she was highly favored, we are all highly loved and prized in God's eyes. Yet God allowed this train of thought to be recorded because He loves and values our emotions—even when we don't realize how wonderful we are in His eyes. Mary sung from her heart, feeling blessed to be thought of so highly by God and honored to carry His Son.

You see, God thought Mary was perfect for the job of mothering His Son. God thought Elisabeth was perfect for the job of mothering the forerunner of Christ. And He made sure they met before they were even out of their mothers' wombs. God was creating divine connections among women and among sons on purpose, for a purpose!

God is an elevator of women—later, Jesus would have many who followed His ministry, and He was very good to women, unlike many in His day. Jesus had the distinct blessing of having such a strong mother of faith. Elisabeth was older and God put her in the life of a younger woman on purpose. Elisabeth understands immediately because when the Holy Spirit fills John in the womb, He simultaneously opens her eyes to the truth. That's why she so loudly calls her the "Mother of my Lord."

Remember that up until this point, the only people who know what's going on are Mary and Joseph—and God really had to help Joseph understand because his mind was flipping just considering everything. God had to send an angel to convince him that Mary was telling the truth. Joseph is a wonderful man. In that time, to raise a boy who wasn't your own as if he was your own was likely very rare. Joseph was such an honorable man.

But notice that God didn't have to convince Mary or Elisabeth— they both immediately accepted His will and agreed with what God had said to them. Mary felt so good about it that she broke out into song. Womanhood itself was being honored, celebrated, and reinvigorated through these two women, and that is, was, and always will be a very good thing.

Chapter 15

Where Eve Failed, Mary Succeeded: She Kept the Faith...and Her Divine Secret

The faithlessness of Eve, who was the mother of all those living, brought us into sin and death. The faith of Mary brought us into redemption from that sin and death and gave us all a future that, if accepted, has the ability to change our lives for the better.

What did Eve do differently from the start? She entertained doubt about God's will for people. What did Mary do differently from the start? She immediately accepted that whatever God's will was, it was a good thing. One questioned the nature of God Himself as good; the other didn't do that at all and only questioned how His will would be done through her. There is a lesson there in the power of not only faith, but also in the immediacy of believing God.

There was no long, overthinking with Mary. There was no "what's in it for me" mentality. The interesting thing is that Eve was living the dream—she was not in a time when men thought little of her as a woman, and she wasn't living under any tyranny at all. Eve was gloriously free and spoken well of; she had more than what she needed in life and literally lived in paradise.

Mary, on the other hand, didn't have it nearly as good. She lived in the sin-sick world that told her she was less than a man, not as good even as male children, and that the best she could hope for was to land a good man, have a bunch of babies, and honor her husband. Eve, on the other hand, had all the time in the world to enjoy her life, and Adam adored her so much that the compliments were freely flowing. Eve saw God, and she still didn't believe in the end. Mary did not see God, but she believed from the start. Eve saw God Himself. Mary saw a messenger of God. Big difference! Still, the faithlessness of Eve didn't affect the faithfulness of Mary.

We all have choices, and the choices we make affect everyone around us. In the cases of these two women, however, their choices changed everything for everyone. We don't have a "sin problem" anymore because of Mary. Because of Mary, we have a "choice solution." If Eve brought us problems, in Mary we find the Answer who gives us all the other answers that matter.

Mary had to hide her divine secret her whole life and was scorned, by those who didn't believe, as a woman who didn't keep herself pure before marriage. She literally took the brunt of societal scorn for the sake of following God's will.

Mary Knew Her Son Belonged to the World and Not Just Her

Mary's first child was a gift to her, and she loved her child—but she knew right from the start that He would not be a mama's boy. She knew He was the Son of God, not only the son of Mary. She kept her divine secret concerning the virgin birth and Joseph maintained his protective stance of his wife, Mary, even after they had other children.

Why don't the Gospels talk much about the virgin birth? Because Mary's virginity wasn't the issue or the focus for Christian faith—Jesus was the focus of Christian faith, and that was on purpose and right. Miracles are interesting and inspiring, but they don't change the lives of other people. Jesus changes the lives of others. The Holy Spirit changes the lives of others.

Remember that after the Day of Pentecost, when the Holy Spirit came down and baptized everyone in the Upper Room with fire, they were all endued with boldness to witness about Jesus Christ. That is really where Christianity took off. It didn't take off because of Mary's sexual status. It didn't take off because Jesus was a miracle child. When the Holy Spirit showed up, everybody in the Upper Room got the Holy Spirit and was touched like John the Baptist was touched—and his boldness became common among believers.

Mary's miraculous impregnation was not enough to build Christianity any more than a leper's skin being miraculously healed by Jesus—the signs and miracles were evidence of Jesus' power on the earth, and Jesus Himself was the focus. Jesus was the embodiment of God and the Holy Spirit, and so it wasn't until He died and rose again, until the redemption plan was in place and the Holy Spirit came down on the believers like fire, that Christianity took off and began to spread. These were regular people having a very irregular experience—salvation and baptism of the Holy Spirit changed everything, and Mary was in that Upper Room experiencing it all just like the rest of them.

The apostles were told to go and preach what they had seen and heard in the life and ministry of Jesus Christ—not in the life of Mary. They weren't told to preach what they didn't know, and, honestly, nobody was there when the virgin conceived at the hand of God. All of those who knew that story had to simply believe it by faith like we do. Mary saw what happened to her, and God sent an angel to confirm with Joseph that she was in fact telling the truth. The Holy Spirit is the One Who told Elisabeth that Mary was carrying the Christ child. Yet that is not the focus of Christianity for a reason. Jesus is the focus because He is the only redeemer we have, and no matter how wonderful Mary was, or Elisabeth was, or John the Baptist, or any of the rest—no matter how great they were, they were not the Son of God.

WHY MARY DID HER BEST TO KEEP HER DIVINE SECRET

Men have seed, and the womb of a woman can be called a cradle—Mary couldn't even tell anyone about Jesus because they would have tried to kill her for being pregnant before the finality of her wedding. I sometimes call the annunciation the magna carta of womanhood because it changed everything for women. The virgin birth is an inseparable part of the person and work of Jesus Christ, but it came at a heavy cost to His mother, Mary. She carried her divine secret all her life. She ran to spend three months with Elisabeth in that time so nobody would know what was going on. Joseph put her away for the same reason—to avoid public scrutiny and possible harm to Mary. They would have called Mary horrible names. She would have been despised.

Mary was betrothed, which, during that time, was a much more committed and contractual bond than our modern-day engagement. In the eyes of others, she was already considered Joseph's wife, but consummation of the union was only acceptable after the final marriage ceremony. This was a time when women were scorned for being anything less than virginal—and nobody would have believed Mary had she told her divine secret. Mary, Joseph, and Elisabeth all knew this, and they hid the secret and didn't broadcast it because it was unacceptable in the time they were living in.

Being an unacceptable woman would have brought not only shame on Mary but consequences for the whole family, including Jesus as well as any other children they had after Him. Now, I've read so many books about whether Mary had other children after Jesus or not—and there are conflicting ideas. My opinion is that if God didn't explicitly say it either way, we should perhaps realize that it wasn't important to God to tell us. I personally don't believe Mary was a virgin forever, and I have my reasons, but I know some feel differently and that's fine by me. We will all find out when we get to Heaven! I do know that Mary didn't go out of her way to share the miracle of her virgin birth of Jesus, though. In fact, she did her best to hide it all the days of her life.

We don't talk much about Joseph, but Joseph was one honorable man. The Word says that God heard him think, and the angel of the Lord came to confirm the miracle to him so that he would stop worrying about Mary. You see, God cared about Joseph too—he was just as chosen as Mary was chosen, because Joseph too would have to carry the secret. He'd have to protect his wife and raise a son he knew was God's own. Imagine what he thought; imagine the weight of that situation. What amazes me is that the scriptures don't say God heard Joseph talk—it says God heard him *think,* and He responded.

God hears our thoughts. He knows our intentions and from where those thoughts stem—and He comforted Joseph with knowledge that Mary was truthful about what had happened to her. And Joseph, as we all know from the traditional Christmas story, was careful to put Mary away so that no one would know of her pregnancy. Mary had a good husband in Joseph, and Jesus had a good earthly father in him, too.

Chapter 16

Should We Pray to Mary?
And if Not, Why?
Should We Honor Her or Not?

The question, "Should we pray to Mary? And if not, why?" is one that I get a lot. Since so many people ask me my opinion about praying to Mary, let's go ahead and get right into the nitty-gritty of it right now. Again, you must understand that I was in the Catholic Church as a kid, and as far as I know, my name is still on the role. Here is my opinion about what I believe is the best way to pray and why, and what I believe Mary would want us to do.

When I was a kid in the Catholic Church, we were taught to pray to Mary—but the whole premise of doing that was because we were led to believe Jesus might not listen to us. It was from a place of unworthiness to speak to Him directly, and also a form of coercion. "He won't turn His mother down, so if you want something, ask Mary," was the line of thought given to me as a child. So, to me, it starts from a place of lack—a place of feeling like we are not really connected to God. This bothers me because I want everyone to know that Jesus came to bridge that gap between God and us, and so we can know in our heart that God always hears us when we pray.

Mary had connection with God. "The Lord is with thee" is what the angel spoke over her at a time before Christ's redemption. She was wonderful, full of grace and faith—but we are told how to pray in the Bible, and this means the Word of God must trump religious ideas and tradition.

Why would you talk to a lieutenant when you can talk to the general? Why pray to angels when you can pray to the Lord? Why pray to Mary or anyone Jesus loved when you can pray to Jesus? Jesus loved Mary, and until the day He died on the cross, He was concerned for her and even gave John the command to treat her as his own mother once He departed the earth. Jesus loved His mother deeply and wanted her taken care of after He was gone. If Jesus had wanted us to pray to her, He would have said so.

Asking Mary to pray for you to Jesus is just putting a middleman between you and God—something God doesn't want. He sent Jesus to create a way that we might be able to draw close to Him in fellowship. There is only one mediator to God, and His name is Jesus. Mary recognized this. If Jesus had been Joseph's baby, He would have just been a great teacher and a prophet, but Jesus was Someone altogether different because He was God. Angels knew it. The earth knew it. God knew it, and Mary and Joseph knew it. I believe if Mary were on the earth today, she would be immediately telling us to please pray to her Son.

DO YOU THINK PRAYING STOPS IN HEAVEN?

We like to think that prayer ends here—because once we cross over, we are with God. But praying doesn't stop here. The Bible says that Jesus makes intercession for us in Heaven even. So, yes, I believe Mary does pray in Heaven, and maybe because so many people feel unworthy to approach God, they choose her out of their own insecurity over God's love for them. This is praying from a mental place of lack, when God's entire purpose in sending Jesus was to draw us close to Him.

God wants us to boldly go to His throne of grace in prayer and ask for what we need (Hebrews 4:16). Jesus preached and told us to pray directly to the Father in His name. We can be humble before God, and should be—but we should also see Him as a real Father and go to Him without reservation.

Do I believe people in Heaven pray? Yes, I do. My mother is in Heaven, and if she is anything up there like she was down here, I'm sure she's bugging someone every now and then to "Watch out for my boy!" Why couldn't she pray for me up there? I imagine that she could and would. There is no scripture that says she cannot.

So, I personally believe that Mary indeed prays in Heaven—but the One Who is going to answer any prayer isn't Mary, it's God. We should do like Jesus said, and not veer from it. If He said this is how you should pray and gave us the "Our Father" prayer in Matthew 6:9-13, then we should see that as a picture and a pattern of what our prayers should be like.

JESUS SPED UP HIS TIME FOR HIS MOTHER

God never corrected Jesus on this earth. He yelled down from Heaven at His baptism, "This is My Son, in whom I am well pleased!" Jesus was perfect and led a sinless life. Jesus gave us the words of life. He was the Way, the Truth, and the Life.

As much as I love Mary, she was human and imperfect in some ways. Twice in Jesus' ministry, Mary tried to get involved and He shut her down, and she listened. He did it once when she was griping about Him being away at the temple when He was twelve—He told her to leave Him be because He was "about My Father's business." He did it again when He was speaking and she tried to pull Him away from it thinking He'd lost his mind—He said, "Who is my mother? Who is my father? Who are my brothers? Those who do the will of God!"

So, Jesus had no problem putting His mother in place and dismissing family hierarchy in favor of God's will. God came first in the life of Jesus because He was here to teach us and redeem us. He knew He only had so much time on this earth, and even His mother would not stop the plan of God from being done in His life. If Mary tried to stop Him from doing what He was called to do, He immediately shut that down. She was not perfect, but she was good—and she listened when Jesus spoke. Mary deferred to Jesus, and we should follow her example in that, too.

It probably pierced her heart when her Son chose His ministry over her words. Wouldn't it make you mad if you had a child and sent word that he needed to stop and come home, and he said, "What? My mama is outside? Who is my mother? *You* who believe what I'm saying are my mother!" Can you imagine hearing that? Mary

probably thought, *I carried you for nine months and this is what I get?!
Don't you talk to me like that, boy!*

Jesus said that because it was true—and He knew that the
separation between His earthly family and His divine calling needed
to happen. He had to walk His life and ministry alone. Mary wanted
to be with Him, of course, and He was with her often. Jesus loved
His mother, but He loved His Father God more. He knew He was
here for a reason, and it wasn't just hanging out eating fish at His
mama's house all the time. Jesus was not destined to have a "regular
life" and He knew it.

Still, Jesus listened to His mother—she influenced Him greatly,
even causing Him to speed up His timeline and perform His first
miracle ahead of schedule. The marriage at Cana is proof that Jesus
loved His mother enough to be flexible in order to please her. Turning
the water into wine didn't stop Him from being about His Father's
business or ministering to people through preaching. He told her it
wasn't yet His time, but He did the miracle anyway. Why? Because
He loved His mother and wanted to please her, and since the miracle
didn't go against anything God had told Him to do, He did it. This
shows us that Jesus is flexible and will even alter His course of action
if it doesn't go against what God has already told Him to do.

I love Mary's response when He agrees to help with the wine.
She turns to others around and tells them, "Do whatever He tells
you to do!" Mary believed in Jesus. She hadn't even seen Him do one
miracle yet, and still she believed in Him. Her faith was strong, and
by telling others to listen to Jesus, she showed how quick she was to
believe.

All Jesus wanted to do was go to a wedding party and have a nice
time. Now, His mother has Him working! By doing it, He's telling
her, "Mama, I'll always be your son and help you" and by putting her

in her place at other times, He's telling her, "Mama, you know I am here to do what God says first."

I imagine that it was a little difficult for Mary to know that there would always be that separation between them—the call of God on His life meant that, like it or not, Mary would have to come second to God. The kind of woman she was, though, it's unlikely she minded that very much. Mary was chosen by God as Jesus' mother for a reason. She had the disposition as well as the faith in God to handle not being first.

LET IT BE DONE ACCORDING TO YOUR WORD, GOD!

Mary's faith was so strong—she was walking in it before the angel ever showed up. She didn't have a special gift of faith; she just lived it and others saw it enough for her to be favored by others and by God. She became the chosen woman among all the others around her— the chosen female of a chosen group of people, and her exaltation rested upon the total surrender of self.

When she said, "be it unto me according to your word," she was resting in her faith that God would not give her more than she could handle and that if He said she should be the mother, then that is what she would be. She just immediately took the position, and her only question was how it would physically be done since she was a virgin. She had no questions about the future or what her life would be like once she said OK to God. She accepted quickly what was asked of her.

Most people are not as decisive as Mary. This was a young woman, and yet her ability to believe quickly and act decisively at the word of God is remarkable. The angel was asking her to believe something totally unbelievable and totally impossible. So, when I hear people try to criticize her, I want to tell them to shut their mouths—because they don't have a fraction of the faith Mary had and the way they are talking shows it!

Do Christians usually say what Mary said, "Be it unto me according to Your word"? Or do they usually say, "Is that really what You mean, God? I don't know; I'll have to think about that a while"?

NO GREAT CAUSE SUCCEEDS WITHOUT WOMEN

All of human advancement requires women. Men need women. Children need women. Women need women! All of us are better for having women at the helm in many areas of our life; but we are especially blessed when women of faith are leading the way because it just seems like women are often quicker to have faith in God. The church is often filled with women, because many women tend to be more open and sensitive to the things of the Spirit. They carry us in their womb; they carry us through life. Houses are often made homes by women—many have that ability to just make a home out of anywhere they might be. It's a blessing!

No great cause succeeds without women—all of our history rests upon them, whether they are given credit for their part or not. Whether they take a lead role or a supportive role in the efforts of human advancement, their contributions and voices are incalculable and invaluable. I love seeing women advance and bust through the old, traditional "man's world" view. I love seeing them rise up and be honored for who they are. God gave this world a wonderful gift in giving us strong women of faith, and Mary was definitely one of the best!

Mary had a track record that brought her favor. When the annunciation came to pass, it was like the magna carta of womanhood to me. Success follows favor, and favor follows faith.

Mary had it all inside her heart before she ever was used by God to have and raise Jesus, and she found the perfect partner in Joseph, who was a remarkable man in his time too. God placed His Son strategically in this family—with a very strong woman of faith and a very understanding man of faith. They could have given up, but they protected Jesus with everything they had in them, listened to the Holy Spirit when He said to move, and stuck with Jesus till the cross and beyond. These were faithful people.

MARY SHED NO BLOOD, MARY SHED HARD TEARS—THIS IS WHY WE HAVE ONLY ONE REDEEMER, AND IT IS MARY'S SON

It gets uncomfortable for Protestants to talk about Mary or her prayers because for so many years they've sought to distance themselves from her—but Mary is a pillar in our faith and important to our faith. She's the person God chose and that makes her special. She was highly favored by God—and because of that, we should highly favor her too. She is an amazing woman who brought honor to all women of faith, but she did not die on the cross for our sins. She is not our Redeemer. Mary needed a Redeemer just like the rest of us, even if she was Christ's mother.

The blood shed on the cross redeems us. Mary shed no blood. Mary shed tears. Mary was at that cross, and it hurt her to the bone to see her Son. Yet He would not allow her to look away. He told her from that torturous place to look at Him! Jesus likely saw His mother breaking down in tears—but that blood He shed was for her too, and He wanted her to see what He was doing. He wanted her to remember Him. "I was born to die, Mama; you know that this is what I have to do," seems like something He might have wanted her to know.

I believe that if Mary were on the earth today, she would not want anyone to take away from her Son's great sacrifice by inserting her into the redemptive work. As humble as Mary was, I believe it would be unfitting in her mind to step into that role—because she saw with her own eyes what it took to take on the sins of the world. She saw her boy hanging on that cross. She saw Him whipped and made fun of; she saw the spear stabbed in His side and the thorns in that crown crush her boy's brow. She was in the Upper Room when the Holy Spirit came down. She saw it all, and if you think she'd want to take His honor in any way away from Him, well you might not know what it means to be a truly good mother.

Mary was a good mama. She is worthy of our praise and honor— but she did not go to the cross to die for our sins, and she cannot be a stand-in for Christ. Nobody took that beating but Jesus. Nobody took that pain and suffering but Him. And we do Jesus Himself a dishonor when we put anybody or anything in that place because He alone bore the sins of the world on our behalf. Jesus loved His mother and she loved Him in return, but they are not interchangeable when it comes to redemption. Each had their role to play and a destiny to fulfill, and aren't we so grateful that they did their part? I'm grateful for Mary's faith and obedience, but I am more grateful for Jesus' sacrifice on the cross for me. I know that you are, too!

So, we should praise Mary. We should honor her for her deep faith and quick obedience. We should learn from her. But we should not elevate her to the level of Christ, and that's all I'm going to say about that!

WHAT CAN WE LEARN MOST FROM MARY?

What can we learn most from Mary? We can learn to say, "Let it be done unto me according to Your word, God!" We can learn to be quick to believe the Word of God—to not overthink and explain it away, but to just accept it in faith quickly and expect that what we read will come to pass in our own lives.

Even if the plan doesn't look right and there are taxes to be paid— we can have faith in God to work it out for us! Even if the plan doesn't seem to look right and there's no room at the inn—we can have faith that, no matter what, God's Word will come to pass and what we are holding inside of our hearts will be born!

If God said His Word is coming to pass, we can choose to believe that with quick Mary-style faith. Whatever dream needs birthing, whatever vision needs to come to pass, or whatever portion of the Word of God we want to see manifest in our own lives, all we need is a little Mary-style faith! We can choose to walk in favor. We can choose to do right because it's right, and not second-guess God.

We can learn from Mary that we too should put God's plan before our personal reputation. It doesn't matter what people say about us; what matters is that we are doing what God said and protecting the vision He has given to us. We do not have to cast our pearls before swine, so to speak, and shout it from the rooftops—from Mary we learn that sometimes it's best to find support in few rather than many. Sometimes it's best to just accept that not everyone is going to understand what God is doing in your life or what He's promised to you. Sometimes you just have to be honored that He chose you for that calling or honored you by giving you that dream or vision for your life. We learn from Mary that it's not important that everybody supports you.

What can we learn from Elisabeth and Mary's divine connection? We can learn that God will send people into your life at times that are "meant to be"—to see what God is doing, and so that you have someone to relate with who understands when nobody else does. Don't dismiss those He puts in your path this way, even if they don't look right for the part. Mary was very young; Elisabeth was much older. They were an unlikely match, and yet, together, they were a divine match of women who needed one another for the role God called them to play in His great plan. Don't forsake friends who believe—they are God's gift to you!

What can we learn from the apostles who kept Mary's secret and didn't speak about it until after she was gone to Heaven? We can learn that sometimes what God does in a person's life does not need to be broadcast if it will cause them harm. God will see to it that His message gets out at the right time—and just flapping your jaws because you know something isn't good. Gossip does no good for anyone. Mary, Joseph, and all who ended up knowing about Mary's divine secret kept it until she was out of harm's way—as a protection over the favored woman of God. This was honorable, and we can be honorable by guarding others who need their secrets kept, too.

I hope these bits I've gathered from a portion of Mary's life inspire you. I hope you start to see yourself in her a little and value her qualities more than you did when you began reading, because Mary was one woman who deserves honor and praise. Her strong faith and quick-to-accept-God's-Word kind of obedience are worth your admiration.

As believers, we should goal to be like Mary in many ways. Let's aim to be so confident inside that God's Word is the best thing for us that when we read it we immediately say, "Good! I accept that, God. I don't know how it's going to happen, but I know You can do anything. Nothing is impossible for You, God, and that means nothing is impossible for me, too. So, let it be done unto me according to Your Word, oh God! I'm ready for whatever comes because I know that You are inside my heart, You are with me at all times, and Your promises will come to pass in my life!"

I AM ALWAYS GOING TO HONOR MARY, AND I SUGGEST YOU DO, TOO!

I'm always going to honor Mary because God honored Mary— and so just like I admire the apostle Paul or any other disciple or biblical figure who had the guts and audacity to believe God, I will admire and honor Mary. We can learn from them all, you know, and we don't have to paint them as just characters. These were real people with real emotions, and they had real faith, too.

It bothers me that we still have so much fixation with Mary, Mother of Jesus' virginity and Mary Magdalene's promiscuity. While I know that God needed Mary to be a virgin for His Son to come—He wanted her body and soul pure before Him—the truth is that God didn't love the Virgin Mary any more than He loved Mary Magdalene who worked on the docks. God loved them both and used them both for His wonderful purposes in the end.

You see, it's only men and other women who won't let you forget your past. God will erase it—blot it out and throw it in the sea of forgetfulness, never to be remembered against you anymore. So, while many still do, I refuse to see Mary Magdalene as some whore down by the docks. When are we going to see that woman for who she really was? That woman was the first evangelist to preach, "He's alive!" after the resurrection of Jesus Christ. *That* is who that woman was!

As believers, when we stand in judgment and keep holding women down in shame when God has forgiven and lifted them up, we are dishonoring God's power to redeem and change anybody. Many people act like the blood of Jesus has a stopping point—but it does not. It flows no matter what a person has or has not done. If we can't forgive and we still label, we are doing a disservice to the blood, and we are only serving to help the devil keep God's women down.

We are meant to lift all people up. God can save a man or a woman and change their lives for good—He is the Master at doing such things, and it doesn't matter whether they are male or female. There is no such distinction in Christ. From our spirit, we are equal in Christ—saved the same, redeemed the same, wanted and loved the same. We are different as male and female, but our spirit is one in Christ!

So, we cannot praise one Mary and cut the other Mary down when God loved them both and forgave them both. The mother of Jesus is to be praised, no doubt—she kept the faith and was known for her faithful actions. But Mary Magdalene is to be praised too because she knew what it meant to be discarded, used up, and thrown away by both men and women who didn't value her at all—and yet Jesus saved her and she became totally new in life. Old things were passed away for her and all things became new when she met Jesus Christ. Many women can relate to that! Let me tell you something, God loves women—and He will reach out and save the ones nobody cares about just as easily as He will reach out and save those whom the world calls "good." So don't let all that fool you! God loves us all.

I enjoy reading about when Mary Magdalene saw Jesus after He rose from the dead. She ran to touch Him (and this is my paraphrase), but He said, "Whoa! Mary, back off! I have not yet ascended! But go tell My disciples and Peter that I am alive!" Mary Magdalene took off running like crazy to spread the message. You see, when you have been delivered and saved from a lot of sin, you have a heart that will run with the message because you know what it means to be forgiven and loved for who you are, regardless of what you've done. If anybody deserves to be honored, it's Mary Magdalene because she's proof of what God can do! Just like Paul, her life was totally changed. The Bible is full of such stories, and they give us hope, don't they? I love it!

So, in close, I just want to say—you gotta be careful with those Marys! Ha! God can and will use anybody who has a heart to serve Him—and Mary, the mother of Jesus, had that kind of passionate heart of faith, as did Mary Magdalene and Elisabeth, too. God has given us examples of all sorts of different types of women in Sarah, Deborah, Ruth, Anna, Martha and Mary, and others, and we have many examples of powerful women of faith in the world today, too. Let's recognize the beauty in each one. It takes all kinds to make the world go round, as they say, but I think it takes women of faith to change the world.

Mary was a world-changer! Learn from her example. Honor her. She's a wonderful example of pure, simple, and obedient faith, and we all could use more of that. Amen? Hail, Mary!

Jesus

The Light of the World, the Hope of the Future...His Story Isn't Finished Yet

Chapter 17

The Miracle of Jesus Christ—Baby in the Manger, God in the Flesh

There is no way to write a full and encapsulating chapter or even book on Jesus Christ—so don't get the idea that this section will come close to scratching the surface of Who God is in the person of Jesus Christ! The New Testament includes so many stories and divine words of wisdom, much more than we will be able to comprehend in our lifetime. We will spend eternity exploring the depth and personality of our Savior, Jesus—the mind-boggling idea of God coming as another so that He could be the Son of Man in order to save mankind. Here in this section? I will share my heart and my thoughts as I thought about God and the baby in a manger so long ago.

Infant Savior—that's really what we tend to see Jesus as during the Christmas season. There are no scriptures outside the birth and Herod's wish to kill Christ within what Herod believed to be the first two years of His life. There are no stories of Him as a child. In fact, it is only at

12 years old that we begin to see the kind of man that Jesus is growing into—and at that age, which the Jews consider a very important age, the age believers call "the age of accountability," we see Jesus as a fierce learner of Jewish religion and tradition with a very clear idea already that His purpose is to be "about the Father's business."

I find it interesting that the word *business* was used. Not ministry. Not charity. Business. I like to think of it in real terms, like the Father sent Himself in the form of His only Son to do a job here on the earth. And so, Christ comes to do that job—and He starts like we all do, in a womb, a protected place. Once He is out, trouble begins but not at His own hand. The fallen spirit-world is disturbed. The stars themselves have told a story about His timing on the planet. And while Jesus' business is God's plan—to bring hope, wisdom, redemption, and the promise of eternal life to mankind—He is not on the ground very long before someone is trying to kill Him. But who cares about Herod? Kings can make all sorts of evil plans. God protects His Son, we know, and the story of man's redemption continues.

Jesus came as a miracle. A baby. Tiny and new, God came and lived as one of us—and yet completely set apart for the business of changing the world.

In nature, all of the animals reproduce after their own kind. Humans are taken care of the longest by their parents. In the wild, animals fend for themselves much sooner than we typically do. Unless you had a parent who abandoned you, and many have had that happen, a good parent is known for taking care of their young ones until they are of age to really take care of themselves. Babies grow up to be teenagers who grow into adulthood and live on their own—of course, today, it looks like a lot of our young aren't going anywhere! I tell parents as a joke, "You might as well give them your house and not just the basement, because it looks like you might be leaving the earth before they start leaving your house!"

It's amazing how powerful babies are! They'll make a grown man dance. They'll make a mother stay up all hours of the night. So, what does a baby need? A baby has to be fed, warmed, held, and cared for down to the littlest detail, and if you don't meet the need, the crying begins. Have you ever noticed that God put a cry in a baby that will draw a mama and daddy out of bed at 2:00 in the morning? That cry will get you, man! It'll cause strangers to even turn around in public and see if you're going to make it stop! Something in good human parents is signaled by that cry to move quick and soothe that baby—to do whatever is necessary to make sure the baby's need is satisfied and peace is back in the house, or in the car, or on the subway, or whatever. Do you think Jesus was any different than a normal baby in this respect? We don't know because God didn't see fit to tell us in His Word.

We do know that manna did not fall from the sky and drop into Jesus' mouth—if so, I believe that miracle would have been recorded, don't you? Mary still had to feed, warm, hold, and care for Jesus as she would for any other baby, but she did that job knowing that He was going to be special in the world. Both Joseph and Mary knew Jesus was going to be a king and called the Son of God. Knowing that, I imagine that they both strove to care for Jesus and raise Him in a way that was fitting of what they were told His future would be. Joseph and Mary were people of strong faith, and they raised Jesus devoutly in the Jewish faith of their family.

JESUS—OUR INCOMPARABLE SACRIFICE

The Bible says that God is a Spirit. Those who worship Him do it in spirit and in truth. Jesus is what happened when God decided to confine Himself to human flesh—to start as a baby, grow, understand us by being us, and move into full adulthood.

Jesus lived to 33 years old. That is when God determined that He did not need to teach or see anymore—it was time for the job He'd come to earth to do to be done. What was that job? The sacrificial death of Jesus for the sins of the whole world. When you see the manger, I hope you see that an incomparable sacrifice was in that manger. There never was nor ever will be another Jesus Christ. God will not repeat the sacrifice because it needs no improvement.

Everything God wanted to experience as a man and do for mankind was done in 33 years—the birth, the childhood, the ministry, the miracles, the cross, the resurrection, the ascension, and, my favorite, the promise to return! Jesus was born to die, and like the scripture says, He was the sacrificial Lamb of God, slain before the foundations of the world. That is very hard to comprehend, but it essentially means that God planned to give Himself before the world even began. This is how God chose to show His love—not passively, but demonstratively.

God is not human. God is a Spirit, and He is far beyond our intellect, and we won't understand everything until we see Him face to face. But, as Jesus, He gave us a much easier way to understand Who He is at His core—taking on humanity, we can relate so much better. Whoever thought God would do such a thing? Even Satan didn't see that coming.

Whoever thought God would leave Heaven to walk on a sin-sick earth and experience this life from our perspective and His own? That's what He did. Even Satan, who regretted killing Jesus on the cross, said that if he'd known what God was doing, he would have *never* crucified Jesus. You see, Jesus was about the Father's business, and nobody understood what was really going on until it was all said and done—until there was nothing Satan or anybody else could do to turn around the redemptive work that Jesus did on the cross.

Jesus was literally born to die. Christmas may be focused on a baby in a manger—but in that manger lays the relatable God Who came to save us all.

"LIVING WATER" IN THE WATER TROUGH

There are no accidents with God—even detours and things Satan does to trap or trip us up, God will use for His own glory. Mary gave birth in the manger because there was no room in the inn—we all have heard that part of the story. What is a manger? It's a trough for water so that animals can drink. Jesus, later in His ministry, referred to Himself as "Living Water"—that all who thirsted and drank of Him would not thirst again. He was speaking about the spiritual thirst we all have and yet sometimes don't recognize.

All people are thirsty before they know Christ. Once we find Him, we have a perpetually filled "manger" of Living Water—so we don't need to go around looking to fill up that thirsty place in our soul anymore because we have the Living Water inside of us. Jesus didn't give us a one-time sip. He gave us Himself. When you see the manger, see that it is for *you* and it will always be filled with Jesus Himself.

Every nativity set has a manger. So, when you see the nativities out and about at Christmastime, I want you to see that manger and think about the child in there as symbolic of the Living Water now inside of you. If you are a believer, I hope you are reminded that nothing can quench the thirst of your soul except the One in the manger.

And if you forget Who is living in you by way of salvation, I pray the Holy Spirit reminds you! If you choose not to drink His Living Water, you will just end up looking for a substitute, and whatever you find will not satisfy your soul. Without the Living Water represented in that manger, anything else is just an empty cup. Even what looks good and sounds good cannot satisfy your soul, because your thirst is always going to be deeper than what artificial water or empty cups can satisfy.

Jesus is not an empty cup. He is not a tiny sip, unless you pull back and refuse to drink in His Spirit. Jesus is a continual fount of Living Water for your soul. This is why, in all areas of our life, we must turn to Him for what we really need—and not accept the substitutes, which are often just the polluted "waters" of the world masquerading as human fulfillment. Let the manger remind you of that!

BINDINGS OF COMFORT, BINDINGS OF DEATH

When the scripture tells us that Mary brought forth her firstborn son and wrapped Him in swaddling clothes before laying Him in that manger, it's telling us that Mary was a good mama. She didn't just throw Jesus in the hay and wish Him good luck; she didn't leave him dirty and cold in the night. No, Mary wrapped the baby in what they called "swaddling clothes," which were just strips of cloth used to bind babies snuggly, to replicate the tightness of the womb and give the babies comfort. People still swaddle today. Sometimes you see mothers walking around with these little burrito-babies—that's what they look like! Wrapped up tight meant Mary was doing what she could to make the baby comfortable.

Can you imagine *God* being comforted? It's amazing to consider what the God of our universe and beyond was feeling or thinking in that moment. Did He choose to forget Himself on purpose and just experience it as new, or did He maintain His Godhood, so to speak, and just watch and feel what it was like to be a newborn? We will not know until we get to Heaven. Man, I'm going to have a lot of questions for God! Aren't you? It's fascinating to think about.

Many see Christ's swaddling clothes as symbolic of what would later be His death wraps. Upon His death, when Christ was taken from that cruel cross, scriptures tell us His body was cleaned and He was anointed with spices, herbs, and oils, before being wrapped in white linen, as was the tradition of the day. One of the oils commonly used was myrrh, which we know was one of the gifts the Magi brought to Him upon His birth. So, many see the swaddling clothes and the myrrh as signs of Christ's future.

When you see those living nativities at Christmastime, I hope you see that myrrh in one of the wise men's hands and remember that what came as a gift when He was a baby would anoint His body after the cross. I hope you look at those swaddling clothes they are wrapping the doll with and remember the wrappings of the real Jesus. Never forget that what bound Him as a child in comfort also bound His body in death—but that no binding whatsoever could keep Him in that tomb. Jesus slipped right through the bindings as He rose from the dead, showing us that hell, death, and the grave no longer have the ability to bind God's children anymore. In that manger was the way out for us.

ANGELS AND COMMON MEN
AT THE MANGER

You'd think the first time the word "Savior" would be used in talking about Jesus would be upon His death, burial, and resurrection, but it was an angel who used it first, and it was right after Jesus was born. The angels were so excited about Jesus that they couldn't help but praise God. In fact, one of them was so taken aback in joy that he revealed himself and spoke to some shepherds who were just minding their own business watching over their flocks. God wanted His Son to be seen by both academics of the time and common men.

The scripture says, *"And there were in the same country shepherds abiding in the field, keeping watch over their flock by night. And, lo, the angel of the Lord came upon them, and the glory of the Lord shone round about them: and they were sore afraid. And the angel said unto them, Fear not: for, behold, I bring you good tidings of great joy, which shall be to all people. For unto you is born this day in the city of David a Saviour, which is Christ the Lord. And this shall be a sign unto you; Ye shall find the babe wrapped in swaddling clothes, lying in a manger. And suddenly there was with the angel a multitude of the heavenly host praising God, and saying, Glory to God in the highest, and on earth peace, good will toward men"* (Luke 2:8-14).

Can you imagine what those shepherds must have experienced, with one angel suddenly talking to them at night and then a multitude of angels suddenly filling up the sky in praise? That had to freak them out a little—this was a new thing going on in both the spirit realm and the physical realm of the earth, and even the angels couldn't help but shout!

Luke 2:15-20 tells the rest of the story of the common men's involvement with the infant Savior: *"And it came to pass, as the angels were gone away from them into heaven, the shepherds said one to another, Let us now go even unto Bethlehem, and see this thing which is come to pass, which the Lord hath made known unto us. And they came with haste, and found Mary, and Joseph, and the babe lying in a manger. And when they had seen it, they made known abroad the saying which was told them concerning this child. And all they that heard it wondered at those things which were told them by the shepherds. But Mary kept all these things, and pondered them in her heart. And the shepherds returned, glorifying and praising God for all the things that they had heard and seen, as it was told unto them."*

These boys had to see what was going on! And, once they saw Jesus, something happened in that manger that made them walk away and start talking about it everywhere they went. What did they see in the infant Savior's eyes? The scripture doesn't tell us, but it affected them so much that they couldn't keep it to themselves—angels had told them, they'd followed the angel's directions, and landed right in the midst of the infant King of Kings. Jesus had just been born, and the life of God was pulsing in that little body. This was no ordinary baby. The shepherds left doing two things—praising and glorifying God—and for what? *"For all the things that they had heard and seen, as it was told unto them."*

The supernatural followed Jesus wherever He went. Angels were watching, as they did during His entire time on earth. Those academic Magi and common men shepherds wouldn't have traveled to see an ordinary baby if the stars hadn't shifted so dramatically and light-filled beings hadn't filled the entire sky. Those kinds of things don't happen in regular life—but they happened around Jesus because He was no ordinary baby.

FIRST SAVIOR, THEN CHRIST, AND THEN LORD

Jesus was a Savior the moment He left Heaven—He had all the ability to rescue mankind residing inside of Him as a baby in that manger. He needed to grow, develop, learn, and teach us, but even the angels recognized that the ability to save was lying in that manger.

When I read the words *"a Saviour, which is Christ the Lord,"* it struck me how they were used. The baby's name was Jesus, but His number one duty was to be our Savior. Then, He is called Christ, and then Lord. Christ means "anointed one," so we know from birth that He was given the anointing to do everything He came to do—and this would develop more and more as He grew. When the angels called Him Lord, they were simply acknowledging the reality of God's authority over it all!

"Jesus is Lord" was the angelic way of telling us that just like God is God, Jesus is Lord—they are in supreme authority, and the angelic host that night couldn't help but praise them for it and let us know, too! It's like hearing, "Hey, humanity! Shepherds, look and listen, and go tell everybody. There is a manger, and in it is a baby who is in authority over everything! Go and see what's happening right now!"

All ability, authority, and anointing was resting in that manger. A preparation for the duties of being Savior was beginning. Right now, all of humanity has the ability to accept or reject the truth about Christ's authority, but it doesn't change the truth. One day, there will be unbelievers or rejecters of the truth who will pay the price for their choice to reject God's plan for mankind. It will be both a joyful and sad day, because while Jesus came to be our Savior, Christ, and Lord, one day He will also be our Judge. Every knee shall bow and every tongue confess the truth that Jesus is Lord. All of Heaven and earth will be in total agreement when we all meet the magnitude of just who inhabited that little baby's body in the manger so long ago. Glory! There will be no mistaking just Who is in authority.

Chapter 18

Jesus—The Inspiration and Illumination of Our Very Existence

What would this earth be without our God's creative hand, without human beings, animals, or any of the rest? It would be like the other planets maybe or like it once was before we came into existence—void and desolate. This earth is teaming with life and possibility, and it is by no means an accident.

If we don't like what we see when we look around this world, it is because the people are spiritually sick and in need of Jesus—who would also later be called the Great Physician. It's not because the world itself is a bad place to be. The evil, the greed, and the morally reprobate actions of people come in because we have an adversary and his name is Satan. Nobody wants to talk about him anymore. Nobody wants to look at the darkness even—we want to pretend as if it's all good. It's not. History itself shows us man's propensity for evil. The further away we get as a society from the purity of Christ, the further we fall into deception and the degradation that follows.

When Jesus came, mankind found hope again. Those who do not want to follow God and enjoy living in darkness are just deceived. As believers, we know that the manger held the hope of the world! Accepting God's plan doesn't change God; it changes us. We suddenly have the hope of a good eternal future and a way to live on earth that is good too. In the manger, we have the Savior we need Who can open our eyes to the truth so that we can see the deception of Satan when it comes. I'll get to more of that in a bit.

Once we release our body in earthly death, something is coming next—like a comma in a sentence, we will pause for a brief moment upon death and move on. Our existence continues and Jesus is the One Who came to illuminate that fact for us. He is the illumination of existence!

What comes after death? It depends. Eternal life, which means being with God, the Source of Life, is what believers who accept God will experience. Eternal death, which means being with God's adversary, Satan, is what those who reject God will experience. One of those two is coming next. Whether people believe it or not doesn't change the truth, and this is what free will is all about. It's not about whether you choose chocolate or vanilla ice cream or whether you pick this or that career—free will is choosing between good or evil, which is God or Satan. The manger is God crying out as a baby saying, "Choose life! Choose life so that you and your seed may live!"

"Choose you this day whom you will serve" isn't a request. We all choose, even if we say we do not because there is no choice not to choose! I know, it's a tongue twister—read it again, ha! Thinking we can opt out is just ego, it's not truth, and atheistic ego is just man's version of Satan's pride.

Christmas isn't just some holiday where you finally get something from your cousins! It's not just an excuse at the end of the year to blow money. Christmas is a celebration of God's rescue mission!

Christmas is God showing us that He didn't mind coming down and walking in the muck of it with us—if that's what it took to save us, He was happy to do it because He thought we were worth it. We are His creation and that's why He calls us His children. He took on humanity to give us hope, as well as to show us how to live good lives. We need God at a core level—not religion!

Jesus was the illumination of our existence because He shone a pure light on what man could be if he remained close to God in daily life. It was a walking, talking example of what a man can be if his spirit is right—if he is connected to God. Until Jesus came, mankind really didn't have much to look forward to outside of this life. Without Jesus, the world was just a puzzle and eternity seemed like a blank. No hope. People were born, and they lived and died without any promise or hope of eternity.

Before Jesus, there was also very little understanding of the devil and the realities of his deceptive tactics upon humanity. Before Jesus, everybody thought everything good or bad came from God or they just looked into the sky and wondered what might be out there. But when Jesus came, all that changed. Truth came! Information came! Hope came! Inside that manger lay the Man who was God—and He shone a bright light on the truth about Satan, sin, and the evil behind the ailments of mankind. He shone a light on what it could mean for mankind to live right, even in the fallen nature of this world.

YOU DON'T HAVE TO WAIT FOR HEAVEN TO LIVE HEAVENLY

Jesus came to teach us that the very spirit of Heaven could reside in us and help us to get our hearts right and live wonderful lives, too.

It's not all about eternal life; salvation is also about living well right here and now, and that begins in the heart.

Even though we still live on a fallen earth, Jesus showed us that we could live as lights in a dark place. We can get what we really need and want in life and show others how to have it too by introducing them to their Maker. You know, at Christmas, people talk a lot about the "Christmas spirit," but what is it really? It's the Holy Spirit having an effect on people. When people let the Holy Spirit flow, they become the best versions of themselves. Love, joy, peace, patience, gentleness, goodness, faith, meekness, and self-control— these are the qualities we end up exhibiting when the Holy Spirit is flowing in us. At Christmas, it seems to spill over onto people you never thought it would.

I love the Christmas spirit. I love that people all over the world are acting more in accordance with God's Holy Spirit. It just makes life nicer! But you don't have to relegate those things to December. One of the most wonderful things Jesus said, in my opinion, was a line He shared in the "Our Father" prayer about God's will being done "in earth, as it is in Heaven." I just love that!

So Jesus wanted us to literally pray for God's will in earth to be the *same* as God's will in Heaven. It begs the question, what is God's will in Heaven? Well, all you have to do is look to the scripture and see—there is no sickness, poverty, misery, hatred, racism, sexism, or spiritual death in Heaven. Everyone knows the truth. Everyone is saved. Everyone has joy and peace, and everyone is the best version of themselves that they could possibly be.

Everyone has everything they not only need but desire. Everyone is flowing in the tangible and wonderful gifts of what could only be described as abundance. The precious metals of our earth are also in

Heaven, and they line the streets and gates. Jewelry and nice things are just normal.

Crystal clear rivers with no pollution are flowing in Heaven. Eternal life is full of the life of God, which means life is teeming everywhere, people are on assignment, and angels are everywhere you look. In other words, it's kind of like the best Christmas you could ever imagine having, where everyone is healthy, happy, smiling, and interacting in love and joy—where you have everything you need and desire in one place, with no evil to speak of. Now, take that and multiply it times a million, and that's God's will in Heaven! And God's will is exactly what Jesus told us to pray for here on earth, too.

What is His will for you? What is His plan in your life? It's that you live the abundant life that Jesus came to give—in whatever manner suits your personal destiny. It will not look the same for everyone because we are all reflections of God's character. Each of us has been given the personality to suit our purpose and the challenge to rise above and see this life as a blessing.

Because of Jesus, we can access God in a purer way—a way that points us always to our best choices, our best attitudes, our best qualities—and that makes life more of a pleasure than it ever could be without Christ. His anointing was in the manger, it was present on the cross, and it is present in us because we are now redeemed. This gives us access to "Heaven on earth" through a total spiritual awakening and total mindset renewal. Christmas becomes an everyday thing—the anointing of Christ in us as we live our lives, overcoming challenges through our faith, learning and becoming the best version of ourselves. God's gift of Christ makes us the gift we give the world.

So you do not have to wait to get to Heaven to live heavenly. You can live heavenly right here on earth—and you can do it without a shred of guilt knowing that this is what Jesus said in His prayer, and it is what the Holy Spirit will guide you to if you let Him. Spiritually, physically, financially, and in every other way, we were not created for poverty. In light of Heaven, there is no tangible earthly abundance that can really compare. On your best day, you will still fall short of Heaven...and yet we are told to pray for God's will to be done "in earth, as it is in Heaven." In obeying that, in growing in our spiritual life, we can turn the natural, limited mindset this world teaches on its head!

FREEDOM FROM IMPOSSIBILITY, FREEDOM FROM "CAN'T"

Life is a ride of sorts, and we get to choose what we think, what we will say, and what we will do. Limited thinking produces limited living. In Jesus, the limits come off because in His eyes, we see a limitless experience of life. We can choose *all* abundance; we do not have to pick just one area as if our God is lacking. He is *not* lacking and He is enough. And because of Jesus, Who came as a man in order to break the curse of sin, guilt, and shame in our lives, we can start thinking, talking, and acting in accordance with abundance.

God is not lacking; so we are not lacking. He is enough; so we are enough. Abundance shows up in our outer world when we are already living it in the inner world of our heart and mind—faith itself is living as if you are already where you want to be, in any and every area you choose to focus on.

What we think, we become. What we say and focus on grows. What we give attention to can either distract us from our best or lead us to our best. We may not always understand the way the path turns in our life, but whatever comes our way we can know that *in* Him we live, move, and have our being—and it all is working out in our favor because Jesus is in us, and through the power and boldness of the Holy Spirit, our eyes can be opened to the best thoughts, the best words, and the best actions we can take. Those three "bests" will take us to our best life, which is always going to be higher than what we see in the world around us.

The world around us will tell us what we "can't" have or "can't" do, but God is great at pointing out what we "can" have and what we "can" do through Christ. The Christmas story is our proof. When everything looked hopeless, God gave us His best in an impossible way. Now, we use His best—Jesus—to create our best selves!

Our best choices in thoughts, words, and actions will stretch us. They will stretch our ideas about what we can do and have in this life. God is in the business of showing us that "impossible" is possible with Him. This takes the limits of our childhood, our experiences up to this point, and the lies the world feeds us every day *off* of our heart and mind so that we can walk *free* from every "can't" of this world. We are free in the spirit first, then our mind, and then our life.

Our faith literally makes us better people if we practice our faith daily and not just on Sunday. How can we do that? Step-by-step, from the moment we rise in the morning—when we give attention to the One Who helps us live out our days with God's heavenly will guiding us. We can't be guided if we don't tune in to hear. We have the Word. We have the Holy Spirit. We should check in with the Word and the Spirit before we check in with anything else. Phones, computers, televisions, and advertisements—these distractions first thing in the morning can pull us away from our best life because they draw us into the details of the natural world.

When we tune into our spirit first thing in the morning, we are tapping into greatness! We are tapping into possibility—an anointing that breaks limited thinking. It's like we are walking into the manger scene, walking to the cross at Calvary, and walking to the empty tomb where shouts of praise are being made. It's as if we are walking in the Upper Room, receiving power from on high with the ancestors of our faith, and that just changes everything first thing in the morning. This begins our day in a way that aligns us with the reason Jesus came—to give us life and that more abundantly.

In the manger was a child who whispers to our heart if we have ears to listen, and He says, "You are not alone...I am with you. If you are heavy laden by life, I will give you rest right in the middle of it. Let Me trade your anxiety for peace, sorrow for joy, disappointment for hope, and darkness for faith. Let Me fill you with the energy of the anointing you need for today, just today. Let Me give you wisdom for your journey that will be as Living Water to you every time you feel a little dry. I am enough, and with Me you will live better and with more joy, peace, and prosperity, too. Whatever good you desire, it's in Me. It's in My wisdom. Come and learn of Me. Walk with Me and see. You do not have to do one thing alone. I am with *you*."

GOD WITH SKIN—JESUS!

Moses tried to get close to God—but even getting near the power of God was nearly deadly. This corruptible flesh of ours could not stand in the presence of such light and power. The energy of God was deadly to the human form. Nobody in Old Testament times could look at God and survive. Yet in Jesus, God became an organic member of the human race—it was God with skin! People could actually hold Him as a baby. Imagine that!

God contained Himself in flesh on purpose. His body was Mary's flesh, but the seed to start life was the Holy Spirit of God. This gave God the ability to experience us and to let us experience Him in a state of being that wouldn't just blow us away! In Jesus, He put aside His heavenly privileges to live as a man.

This is how God could be so acquainted with the pain of being human in a fallen world and why, as Jesus, He was so compassionate toward the lost—He saw and felt it all very up close and personal.

Jesus knew what it felt like to be hunted—He wasn't on the ground for very long before Herod was sending people to try and kill Him just because He existed. Jesus knew what it felt like to be talked about and scorned—everyone wondered about the timing of His birth, and if He really belonged to Joseph. He knew what it was like to be thought of as "less than" the others.

Jesus knew what it was like to be tempted by the devil with everything God promised to Him—sustenance, protection, and a kingdom—and the temptations of Christ wouldn't have been called temptations if they weren't tempting! Jesus was tempted with all the things we are tempted with, the Bible says, and yet did not fall for it. You must remember that Jesus knew Satan before He was even born, but Satan couldn't identify Jesus in the body He came in—and yet he still gave it his best shot to take Jesus down, as he did with so many of the other prophets.

Jesus knew what it felt like to lose those He loved. When John the Baptist died, it was hard on Jesus—He loved His cousin, and the death was so senseless. But Jesus' immediate response was to get up and preach. In other words, even though His heart was breaking inside for the loss of His cousin, He wanted to honor John the Baptist, the most fiery preacher who ever preached, by doing what John did. Jesus went out and reached people with the message of

God. Do you think He was hurting a bit when He did it? You better know it.

I could go on and on about the things Jesus experienced in order to fully feel the weight and strain of being human in a fallen world, but the point is this—we do not love and serve a God Who doesn't know what we are going through. Whatever we encounter, the root of it is something Christ knows and felt and conquered. And because we have Him as our Savior, we can overcome anything that happens, whatever the devil throws, and come out on the other side with flying colors! There is nothing this world throws at us that we can't overcome through the blood of the Lamb and the word of our own testimony.

THE WORLD IS A PUZZLE AND ETERNITY IS A BLANK WITHOUT JESUS

With Jesus, we have core knowledge of who we are, Whom we belong to, and where we are going when we breathe our last breath. You see, without Jesus, this world is a puzzle with missing pieces. Without Jesus, eternity is a blank—a hopeless nothingness. Without Jesus, the morality of man continually spirals to emptiness—a vain searching for only pleasure in trying to find what is really good in life. Without Jesus, social life is a hollow shell—people try to identify with others in an effort to know themselves, to find themselves, and to enjoy themselves. If you do not know who you are, it's difficult to be at peace with anyone else.

Like a man who looks in the mirror and walks away forgetting in a moment what his face looks like, so people without spiritual connection to God through Christ go through life trying to remember who they really are inside. Identity is a core need for people, and they will seek for it in the wrong things just to feel some kind of "knowing" to describe who they really are inside.

Only God holds the true mirror, and in Him we see our reflection in a much brighter light of truth—because in Christ, we find out that who we are is perfect in God's eyes and redemption brings it out in a pure way. Without sin clinging to us, we can be our true selves and not some image trying to compensate for the lack in our own hearts.

God knows us because He made us, and He did not make a mistake. Part of salvation is just finding out who you are in relation to Whom you came from—you are a spirit created by God. That is who you really are and who you will continue to be once you pass into eternity. Don't let the devil and this world skew your identity. Confusion creates all sorts of problems that don't even need to be there. In that manger came a baby who would forever change the world because hope and salvation are necessary in order for mankind to know who they are and to thrive in the life they've been given. This life is a vapor. Our spirit lives forever! So which is more important to focus upon in life? Which will have the most longevity?

Who we are is not a hair color, a body shape, an age, or any external thing we can manipulate or change—and who we are is not even what we do. Who we are is something special! We are all unique in God's sight, a soul different from all the rest, and He did this on purpose. Why do you think the devil wants to tear people down so much—to make them feel "less than" and "not good enough" all the time? Why do you think he pushes people away from Christ? He doesn't want people looking to Christ because he knows they'll find out who they really are. The blinders on their eyes will be lifted and so will their heart. They'll see the power inside of them that God has planted there from the beginning—and they'll know it's for the purpose of living great lives and changing the world for the better in the process.

It is in the devil's best interests that man is confused. He is the author of confusion—and he will try to confuse people about who they are in an effort to thwart the progress of human beings and the progress of humanity. Everything becomes a puzzle with missing pieces. Social life becomes hollow and shallow. Intellectual life becomes idle chatter that means nothing in the end. A life of faith grounds us in truth and not chatter.

A life of faith grounds us in our true identity because we see ourselves in our purest state when we peer into God's mirror—a spiritual state of being that loves this life and has the ability to thrive and overcome anything, including the confusion of the world.

A life of faith opens our eyes to the value of others making social life deeper and richer—we begin to realize that all of life is about relationships, and our relationship with the Lord becomes the foundation with which we can really value all the others.

A life of faith makes our intellectual life a richer experience. We start expanding the capabilities of our mind from a place of soundness. When fear goes, faith grows and the mind becomes a soaring place. Faith adds to intellectual life because when the soul is settled, the mind is freer to expand.

Chapter 19

The Growing Pains of Christ and Christmas

At Christmas there's more hope flying around in the atmosphere than at any other time of the year. Do you ever notice that? I like to say that the hope of Christmas always is "the best is yet to come"—because when Christmas comes, I notice that hope just surges everywhere I go. The birth of Jesus has given us that kind of hope and it makes our horizons seem wider—we dream more, we wish more, and there is so much to smile and hope for.

For a few moments in December, even unbelieving people seem to go out of their way to do more kind acts of service for others. There is more giving, of course, but there is also more cooperation. I love it. The same guy who might have sped ahead of people at the mall to get in the door first in October just may feel an inkling to open the door and let five people go ahead of him come December. Sometimes you just have to call that kind of thing what it is—a Christmas miracle!

As believers, we know that God's best was given in Jesus Christ and that means, now, *our* best can come too—but what happens when we don't act our best on the holiday that represents everything we say we stand for? What happens when our desire to maintain the "reason behind the season" goes a little too far?

FIGHTING ABOUT JESUS—THE EXACT OPPOSITE OF WHAT CHRISTMAS IS ABOUT

Growing pains as a Christian can get all the way down to the little things of life—because, often, how you treat other people can make or break their opinion about Jesus, especially at Christmas. The controversy over whether to say "Merry Christmas" or "Happy Holidays" was raging for a while there, and it really was sad to me.

Lately, I notice a shift back to "Merry Christmas," which blesses me. I guess the controversy didn't need to last very long, although, even today, people can really get in an uproar about it—and some of the ways I saw people acting made me think, *I'm not sure Jesus would have been getting in a fight in the parking lot over this...I mean, I can't see Him taking off His sandal and smacking some lady in the head for screaming 'Happy Holidays!' while ringing her little silver bell.*

I love to hear "Merry Christmas," but if I don't, I don't worry so much about it because I know that I carry Christ with me wherever I go in my own heart. Besides, most of the year those stores don't care about Christ at all, so I guess I just wasn't surprised that they'd continue to not care at Christmastime either! Look, if someone wants me to have a happy holiday, well, I'll take that too—I like all my holidays to be happy! But there is just something better about being wished a Merry Christmas—I like that word *merry* so much better.

I have friends who aren't Christians and they still have no problem telling me "Merry Christmas," just like I have no problem telling them "Happy Hanukkah." Anything that will wish joy upon someone is good to me, but I know that there is no greater joy in the world than Jesus Christ.

"Joy to the world, the Lord is come," you know? The Christmas songs are playing everywhere at this time of the year and I'm just glad to hear the word *Lord* or *Christ* at the mall or in the shops on the street! Whatever we can do to bring the joy of Jesus, well, I think we should do that.

The growing pains of being a believer is sometimes realizing that fighting for something shouldn't come at the expense of what you actually believe. I don't want to get into "fighting about Jesus" because that's the opposite of what Christmas should be about! This is a time of love, peace, and joy—good will toward *all* men and women, and not just the ones who believe exactly like we do. Sometimes in our haste to honor the joy and peace of Christmas we bring exactly the opposite into our interactions with others. We have to be careful of that.

GROWING IN GOD ISN'T ALWAYS COMFORTABLE—IT MEANS STRETCHING OURSELVES TO REACH FOR OUR BEST...EVEN AMONG "THE WORST"

Pride shouldn't be mixed in with Christianity. I've learned a lot of things in the Bible and it's a blessing, but one of the areas I really guard myself in is being prideful about it. That is at odds with Christ and everything He came to give and teach us. It's another growing pain thing when you realize that no matter how much you learn and how much faith you grow in, you are never supposed to feel like "you've got it." There's always room to grow in faith. We will be learning for all of eternity—and our responsibility is simply to grow and share what we've learned so that others can grow, too. It's a place of humility and confidence in Christ, which, believe it or not, is supposed to fit together in all of us.

Jesus wasn't born to give us supremacy over others—He was born to give us supremacy over sin. Jesus didn't redeem us and deliver us so that we could look down our noses on the "unredeemed and undelivered." This is opposed to the message of Christ, and yet sometimes believers get carried away. Growing in God isn't always comfortable; it requires that we continually assess ourselves to be sure that we don't ruin our message with pride. We've got to stretch ourselves to reach for our own personal best, even if we are living among people we consider "the worst."

Jesus didn't give us His teachings so that we could turn around and criticize others for not believing them. It is up to each person what they will accept and believe, and whether it raises their lives up or tears their lives down, their choices are their own. Our responsibility as believers isn't to coerce people into Christianity; it is to share the message of Jesus and the love and goodness of God.

We can't become so staunch in wanting better for people that we end up prideful about what we've learned—we just have to be humble before God, keep learning, and keep reaching for our best thoughts, words, actions, and life!

I Refuse to Become Conceited About What I've Learned

I don't ever want to be conceited about what I've learned or argue with people who don't see things my way. I have opinions. I have ideas. I realize other people do, too. My life is a product of my own thoughts, words, and actions—which began to turn around the moment I accepted Christ as my Savior. The manger held the hope of the world, but until I accepted Christ, it was just an empty display at Christmastime that meant nothing to me. It was just decoration.

Some people will reject the message in the manger. I know that. It hurts me to see people choose what is wrong, when I know that there is so much better. But I refuse to argue religion because that is not indicative of what Jesus did for me! Accepting God's plan through Jesus didn't make me more religious, it made me free—free from sin on a spiritual level, and free from the self-destructive habits of living a rudderless and godless life of work and whim. Life was hard before Jesus. Jesus makes everything easier because the heart is lighter and freer, and not just calmer but more peaceful. There is a difference! I just refuse to live swinging a Christian bat, so to speak, at anyone who disagrees with my beliefs.

So if someone tries to argue with me, I often tell myself, "Jesse, they have a right to be wrong!" Ha! It helps me to make that joke sometimes. Seriously though, I just have accepted the fact that not everyone is ripe or ready for Christ. And even if everybody in the whole world were to accept Jesus, everybody is not going to suddenly think like me, believe like me, talk like me, or live like me. We all tend to focus on what we need in the Word most—and we tend to grow in the areas we focus upon. We get good at what we practice, regardless of what it is, and that also comes to what we focus on in the Word.

As a minister, I know that I can point people to Christ, but it is up to them to *want* the goodness in Christ—and I pray that the Holy Spirit draws them, but my job is just sharing the message. Just like it's not my job to argue about Jesus, it's also not my job to try to make everybody like me...even at Christmas! I smile and spread the joy I've got, and I just hope that others feel the sincerity of my heart and don't get stuck on the lies of the media. But if they do, well, I just keep on keeping on! I have to. I have no other choice. My love for God and my joy for living this life propel me to do what I'm here to do.

I know that God's best is for me to learn my whole life through and I can't do that with a prideful heart—so I refuse to become conceited about what I've learned. If someone doesn't want to hear what I say, they have that right. If they don't agree, they have the right to disagree with me. I have that same right. I wish we all agreed that God is good, Jesus brings hope, and that abundant living is what Christ came to give us. I think life would be better if we all had faith, all lived more lovingly, and all just plain wanted better for each other.

I think we could work together easier if we preferred one another more often and didn't see the world as a dog-eat-dog place. It's only that way because so many people act that way. I see far too many people tearing other people down, and far too few people building others up these days. But at Christmas, there is almost like a pause button that gets hit. There is a pervading atmosphere of "good will toward all mankind" that I just love, and I think as believers, our responsibility to God is to keep that love and joy going throughout the year. What good is it if we are kind at Christmas but jerks come February?!

FATHER JOSEPH, MOTHER MARY, OR FATHER GOD? JESUS—LETTING GO OF EXPECTATION TO FOLLOW GOD'S PLAN

Joseph was a phenomenal man. Would you believe your girlfriend if she came to you and said she was pregnant and that it was an immaculate conception? Would you need an angel to help you with accepting that, like Joseph? Would you hide and protect that woman and the child you knew was not your own? Would you raise that child as your own anyway? Joseph was a very, very good man. He was Jesus' earthly father figure and he watched over Christ as baby, as a boy, and watched Jesus become a man—in the end, his "son" became his Savior. What a wonderful man Joseph must have been to be able to handle all of that and know that he didn't have one biological part in Jesus Christ.

Jesus talked about "the Father" over and over throughout His ministry—He continually pointed people to God, as their Father, showing through His own life example that the Father's business was His main priority. Now, Joseph was a wonderful father, but no man or woman can take the place of Who our soul really needs—*the Father*, who is God.

Everyone knows it's the parents' responsibility to teach and guide a child—but most people leave most of that job to the mother. Women take the lion's share of responsibility in raising children, but it's not right. So many men today refuse to be fathers—they just won't take the responsibility—and I believe that is a big problem today. We need strong men, yet the world sends mixed signals about what it means to be a man. So now we have generations of people who see women taking on both roles and do not understand what an earthly father really is like at all. They have no frame of reference when they hear the Church talk about God as a Father either.

Joseph is an active father. Before they ended up in that manger, Joseph did all he knew to do to find a place for Mary to have that child—remember there was no room at the inn, but Joseph tried. That means he had money and he was trying everything he knew to do to protect and provide for Mary. He knew Jesus was coming. Joseph wasn't the kind of man who cuts and runs. Joseph was steadfast!

When God speaks through angels to Joseph, he listens. When God warns him to move because Herod is about to start killing babies, Joseph gets up and moves quickly. When God warns him to stay away, Joseph does it. Now, remember—this is not his baby! He really has zero obligations to Jesus. All he has are angelic visits, dreams, and trouble! Jesus brings stress into his life, but Joseph takes it and does well anyway because that is the kind of man he is— Joseph loves and honors God. He's a working man, a craftsman in the carpentry trade, and he is a natural born protector and provider. Joseph is more than just a good guy; Joseph is a great man.

Joseph wants his son to have a trade. Since he has no idea when or how the angel's words will play out in Jesus' life, he decides to help His son earn money. By teaching Jesus carpentry and stone masonry, Joseph is trying to give Jesus a future by making Him part of the family business. Joseph doesn't yet understand that Jesus is about to make an eternal future for everyone, including Joseph, by sticking to His heavenly Father's business.

There comes a time when a child begins to make choices that begin to steer him on the path he's chosen—and so even though Jesus had a wonderful mother and father, it's at twelve years old that He really begins to show that He is off-the-charts gifted in His understanding of Jewish religion and tradition. Jesus spends as much time as He can at the temple, listening and talking with Pharisees and Sadducees, etc. By twelve years old, Jesus has an understanding of the Fatherhood of God that we all need to grasp a lot more than we do—and He is so wise beyond His years that He is always astounding His teachers. Can you imagine trying to teach Jesus?

When Jesus goes missing for three days, it's interesting to see that only Mary is really angry—she's mad, and yet she's the one who lost Him! I think Mary was getting to that point most mothers get to, where she sees her boy is growing up and she doesn't really want to let go. Mary would have probably liked it if Jesus had stayed in the manger. Now, Jesus is in the synagogues and streets, talking with the religious minds of the day—and blowing them away.

You see, it doesn't matter how good your parents are, there comes a time when you make your own way. Jesus makes it perfectly clear that His way will be God's way at twelve years old when, after being "lost" for three days away from Mary, He responds to her fussing with, "Woman, I am about my Father's business!"

Now, I'm sure that didn't make Mary too happy! But Jesus will not be scolded for putting God first. Jesus recognizes the authority of God extends beyond earthly authority, and in the Jewish tradition, by twelve years old, He knows He is supposed to be a man even in the eyes of His mother. That He isn't treated that way shows that Mary is having a hard time letting her boy go—but go He must. A separation from childhood things and a preparation for ministry is beginning for Jesus, and it's necessary for His future and for ours.

It's not always a smooth transition from childhood to adulthood. It's definitely not always a smooth transition to move from the expectations of others to the future you have in God. It often requires boundaries that are hard to make, but necessary.

Jesus came to a point where He had to make a decision about which He was going to follow—would it be Father Joseph, Mother Mary, or Father God? Jesus chose God, of course, because God is who He'd need in the future. I'm sure it wasn't easy for Joseph and

Mary. It's never easy for any parent to let go of their time being the primary guiding force. It's also not easy to let go of expectations. I'm sure Joseph would have liked having Jesus in the family business just as much as Mary would have liked having Jesus in the house all the time—both would have probably liked knowing where He was at all times.

No matter what Mary and Joseph's plans for Jesus may have been, Jesus knew He had to please God. To be the Light of the World and the Savior of mankind, Jesus had to sometimes say "no" to the wishes of those He loved. You may have to do the same thing. Jesus didn't stay in the manger, and He didn't stay in His family home forever either—He wouldn't forsake His calling and neither should we.

When you see the manger around Christmas this year, realize that it represents a tiny portion of time. It's Mary's time with Jesus; it's Joseph's time too. It's when God in Heaven was throwing an angelic party in the sky. That didn't last forever. Nothing lasts forever. Babies grow up, boys leave home, and destinies begin when we have the courage to leave the familiar—because sometimes getting "lost" in your mission is exactly what you need to do to prepare for it.

Chapter 20

Jesus—He's for Us, in Us, and Working Through Us Around the World

I love seeing babies. Babies usually love seeing me. I think it's partly because of my white hair that makes me look like I could be their grandpa. Mostly, though, I believe it's the spirit of God inside of me that signals to them that I'm one of the good ones, ha!

Babies are fascinating little creatures. A lot of people can't stand being seated by a baby when they go to a restaurant but not me. I love it! It doesn't bother me if they cry or holler a bit or talk a little too loud. Why does everybody else get to talk at the table but the baby? Man, there will be a table full of people just yacking and laughing loud. Nobody cares. The minute a baby cries out or talks too loud, people start giving the stink-eye—they start looking around like they're ears are offended. I want to say, "You were just talking! Let the baby talk, too!"

Not long ago I was in another mall just walking around with my wife. I stopped, and there was this lady nearby with a baby who was about nine or ten months old. He was crying hard. His face was all swollen up from it. My wife was doing something, I can't remember, but I was stopped right by the little guy. He looked at me and I looked at him, and he just reached his little arms right out to me like, "Hold me, Mister! Please!"

I thought, *I don't know these people. I don't know if they want that, little man!* I didn't know what to do, but I put my hand out toward the child anyway. When the mother saw the baby wanted me and I didn't mind, she handed him right to me. The lady was glad to give me the baby! She was flat exasperated from the crying. They were having a tough time.

Immediately, the baby stopped crying and just smiled. He put his little head on my chest, and so I patted him on the back to comfort him. Mama looked flat shocked. She said, "He doesn't do that." I thought, *Uhhh, he just did, lady.* I decided to tell her the truth.

"He sees Jesus in me," I said.

"Who?"

"Jesus," I said. We had a short conversation, but I could see there was no room in her heart for Jesus. She was just glad an old grandpa was willing to take a shift so she could catch a break. But, while Mama wasn't interested in God, that baby sure was drawn to Who was inside of me. I've been on this earth for a lot of years and I can tell you that children can be very sensitive to the Spirit of God. They can sometimes know more than their parents because they have an instinct that simply draws them to what is good—they can't help themselves. They are looking for joy. I've got plenty of that, but not because I'm some funny man. It's because the joy of the Lord is in me.

Jesus has changed me. I was a mean and angry man before I met the Lord as a young man. People may cut me down, but they don't know how far I've come. It doesn't matter, because my past is gone. In Jesus, I was forgiven and He never brings up that old junk. In Jesus, I was healed. Because of Jesus, I was able to let go of the harshness of my upbringing and just become who, I imagine, I was always supposed to be—joyful, strong, generous, and a comforting place to land for people who need some help. That boy sure needed some joy! He needed someone to lean on. God set us up to be in each other's path—because now, that little man is in this book! And I left him with a gift in the spirit that I hope he feels today, wherever he is.

It's amazing to me how the anointing of God works. As I was holding that boy, I thought, *I need to pray over you.* I didn't want to freak his mother out, so in my heart I just silently talked to God and prayed, "Lord, put my spirit of joy in this baby. Let him receive what I've got inside that he's responding to right now, oh God, because evidently Mama doesn't know what's going on here."

You see, God is always putting what we need on our path—but sometimes we are like the mama, clueless to what is needed, and sometimes we're like the baby, open-hearted enough to see what we need and reach for it.

The more sensitive we are to our own needs, the easier it is for us to be fearless in reaching out. Just like that baby who was needing joy, comfort, and the anointing of God to lift his spirits, we can look to Jesus to get what we need the most, when we need it the most. I see the manger at Christmas and it reminds me of all that Jesus has done for me—spiritually, emotionally, in my body, and in my whole life experience. I was going one direction, but He saw me and I reached out to receive what He had—immediately, what I needed, when I needed it most, came rushing in. Like that baby, my heart lifted. I rested for a minute on Him, and our relationship has just been growing sweeter as the years go by.

What was my number one need way back then? I needed forgiveness, because I knew I was holding on to junk that I could no longer carry—I needed love, I needed forgiveness, and I desperately needed peace. I didn't expect to get joy, but I got that too! You see, we need to unload our junk onto Someone Who can take it, will hold us and comfort us, and put what He's got into us! When we let go and rest on Jesus, He will pick us up and lift our spirits.

We don't sing "Sad to the World" and "It's the Most Terrible Tiiiime of the Year!" We sing, "Joy to the World" and "It's the Most Wonderful Time of the Year." Why? Because we want joy and wonder and all of the rest of the good things in life. We need the good things even in the bad moments. Our hearts are crying out for it. And it's in that Person Who came as a baby, lying in a manger, that we find what our hearts really crave.

In Jesus, we find the forgiveness we need, the clean slate we need, and all the wisdom and teaching we will ever need for creating a good life that's worth living. That is what Jesus brings, because in Him we find a personal Savior Who understands what we need, and when we need it—and He's always right there whenever we reach out to Him.

THE PROCESS OF UNDOING THE CURSE

The curse of sin that came to man with Adam and Eve was all about work, desire, childbirth, and an inequality between the sexes. That's what Satan gave. He promised freedom but gave us the opposite. It's exactly his *modus operandi* today, because that's all he's got—lies. Satan has no new tricks. Every generation, he just puts a different spin on the same old lies.

Redemption from the curse is what Jesus brought and it was marked by true freedom at a spirit/soul level. In Christ, everyone becomes equal—male, female, Jew, Greek, and Gentile; we are all equal in the anointing of God. We were always equal in God's sight, but when our sight was blurred by sin, we began to act in ways that can only be described as despicable. But you do something long enough, you start to not see a problem with it. That's how people end up really messed up in life—they begin small, and whatever their issue, it just grows until it takes over their life. Then, they are living in a reactionary mode from a wounded place of hard living, striving, warped desires, pain, and anger at the inequality seen throughout the world.

In Christ, we are forgiven and the curse is lifted, but we have to walk with God to have what God promises—it isn't like we're floating on cloud nine with grapes dropped by angels into our mouths. Evil still exists. We live in a fallen world; but we are not fallen people anymore. We have been reborn at a spirit level, and now we begin the process of living on a higher level. It happens choice by choice. If we fall, we ask for forgiveness and move on to make a better choice knowing that we've already won in Christ—and as we follow Christ, we see the manifestation of that winning!

The undoing of the curse began with Him, but we live it out each time we choose God's way over this world's way—that's how our lives get so much better. It's not mind over matter; it's spirit over flesh! Our heart can feel clean as we go because forgiveness is always available, but we have to want it and stop frustrating the grace of God by deliberately ignoring His promptings and continuing toward what is self-destructive. In Jesus, we find courage to look at ourselves and let go of what so easily causes us to stumble. Once we see a problem, then we know that our solution is in Jesus—because He will reveal the root and then uproot it.

If we stay curious and close to Christ, we can look at ourselves through His eyes of love and forgiveness, we can let go of the root causes of our habits and be free in our mind. We're already free in our spirit. It's in our daily practice of being open to God's Word and His Spirit that we become part of the process of undoing the curse in our own lives. It's been broken over our spirit and our life, but we have to renew our mind to it—because the old ways are ingrained in our brain, but in Christ we are made new and able to do what we could never do on our own. He helps us to make radical shifts in our outlook on life. He helps us to identify thoughts that just don't suit our new life—so that we can really, once and for all, let them go.

THE HOPE OF THE WORLD—IN US AND THROUGH US

Hope came into the world so that the world could have hope—and we need hope, don't you think? We need it every day. In the Word, we find so much of it and it's the key to the Christmas spirit remaining in us on a daily basis. That same joy of the season is in Christ Himself. That same intimate sincerity is in Christ Himself. That same love and hope for humanity itself is in Christ, and when we live in Christ, we become the ones who bring it to the world.

At Christmas, people around the world suddenly become more generous and loving to those who are in need. As believers, we know that we have become the hands and feet of Jesus at all times of the year, not just when "it feels good" because silver bells are ringing.

Christmas reminds us, though, that the heart of God pulses in us too, and we act more like Christ when we are always looking to help, to serve, and to give some kind of love everywhere we go. That's our mission as believers: to spread the message that God so loved the world that He gave His only Son, and that whoever believes on Jesus can and will be saved—saved from the curse of sin and death, and from all the lies and trappings that surround those two horrible things.

Jesus came as a vulnerable child lying in a manger—and somebody owned that manger and all those animals. Somebody gave Jesus a place to lay His head when the innkeepers just couldn't do it. I think, at Christmas, it's just easier for many people to open their hearts and be that "somebody" who gives, takes in, and helps another human being in need. As believers, though, that's our joy, right? It's our joy to give to the world "as unto the Lord" all year long!

JESUS' BIRTH DRIES OUR TEARS— IF YOU'VE LOST A LOVED ONE, YOU CAN STILL HAVE A GOOD CHRISTMAS

At Christmas, family is such a focus that we can't help but think about and miss our loved ones who have already gone on before us to Heaven. In fact, many people get very depressed at Christmas because they feel the loss so greatly at this time of year. It's true that one of the hardest things we will ever experience is the death of someone we love—but because Jesus was born, we have an enduring hope that we will see them again.

Death loses its former sting in light of eternity. The closer we get to the Lord, the more we realize the truth of eternity. We will miss them being in our everyday life, of course! But we don't just *believe*, we *know* we will see them again—and we will see them young, healthy, and just beaming in the light of Heaven. They aren't "lost" because we know exactly where they are!

I like to say that my loved ones aren't in my past; they are in my *future*. That just soothes my soul. It's a real abiding truth that has helped to dry my tears. I know when I see my mother again, I'll see her like my daddy saw her when she was young and healthy, full of life and spunk! I know that Heaven does not work on the timeframe of earth—if a thousand years is like a day, my mother has been in Heaven just minutes, really. What she is seeing is blowing her mind. The people who went before her whom she loved are there, too.

I'm not sure God knows what He's getting with that many Cajuns in Heaven…but I do know the food is going to be great! That's a joke, but I know you understand what I'm saying. Every person who passes on to Heaven makes it that much sweeter of a place. God loves us, and we bring our personalities with us when we go. We just lose all the heaviness of this earthly body and the weight of sin that permeates this earth, too. We don't realize how much it affects us. I believe we got so accustomed to feeling it that we just considered it normal, but it's not normal.

When we get to Heaven, the love of God in such close proximity has an effect on our soul—we are light-hearted, with zero fear, and there is no more need for faith. Christ is right there, and we can see Him face to face, just like we can see all our loved ones who died here on the earth.

Angels and humans living side by side and moving around freely—God has some special things in store for us! When we start to get a divine perspective, death really loses its sting. When we get a divine perspective, we read scriptures like, *"To be absent from the body is to be present with the Lord,"* and realize that there is no such thing as real death. The body wears out but the spirit lives forever, and when we cross over, it's a sweet and joyful reunion.

If you've lost loved ones, don't let the Christmas season drag you down into despair—realize that the devil would love to sift you like wheat, to steal your joy, kill your hope, and destroy the goodness of this celebration. You don't have to feel guilty for being happy or live holed up in your house to avoid other people who are happy.

Realize that the baby you see in the manger everywhere you go, all those decorations, and all those twinkling lights are reminders that eternity exists and the Maker of it came down to give us all a way to move right to Heaven when we cross over. When you see the manger, thank Jesus for coming because He's the reason why any of us will see our loved ones in Heaven again. He's the reason! Not just for the season, but for eternal life—which gives us that beautiful and truthful promise.

Your loved ones aren't "missing" or "lost" or anything of that nature—they are safe and happy in the light of Heaven and they know you will be there soon enough, so they aren't worrying or fretting. They aren't even hurting or worried. So don't take on hurt and worry that you don't need. Miss them, but don't let that missing steal your joy. You may be young and you may live to be 120 years old, and those years on earth are still *nothing* by Heaven's eternal standards. This life is a vapor and some seem to go too soon, but if you've accepted Jesus, you have the promise that you will be with your loved one again.

I was born in 1949, and it's as if the years have flown by. When I was young, I didn't feel the years went as fast as they do now. So what! I enjoy every year. I make my days good days. I look forward to seeing my family, but I also look forward to the people I have in my life right now. I know Jesus, and so I know I'll see every one of my loved ones who have passed away in Heaven. It's a real place, and because Jesus came, we can go immediately when we take our last breath.

Because of Jesus, my tears are dried in His promise and His great love. If you find yourself hurting this holiday, please, I encourage you to remind yourself of the truth and let Him dry yours, too! He's ready and able to do it so you can enjoy your days and all your holidays, too.

DEATH JUST ISN'T WHAT IT'S CRACKED UP TO BE

Satan wants the sadness to stay. He wants the sickness to remain. He loves poverty and seeing God's creation in turmoil. When Jesus came, He didn't put sickness on people—He healed. He didn't reduce people to poverty—He brought abundance everywhere He went. If the people came to a meeting and were hungry and nothing was close to buy enough food to feed them all, He'd just miraculously multiply what was there. Jesus fed over 5,000 people that way—that's abundance.

If you went fishing with Jesus, He'd nearly sink your boat with the catch by telling you where to cast your net. If you needed money for your taxes, He'd produce gold coins in a fish's mouth. People couldn't even die around Jesus. He'd raise them from the dead and ruin the whole funeral. I know how people can be, and I just bet there was somebody griping at Lazarus' tomb, saying, "I already paid to wrap the guy, I already paid for the flowers!" Jesus didn't care because life was wonderful to Him. He never left anyone with less than when He came. He always left people with more. More wisdom. More truth. More love and peace. More healing. More miracles. More of whatever was needed at the moment.

Everywhere Jesus went, He spoke on having faith in God—on being close to the Father, on prayer, on how to receive, and how to live God's way. He said we didn't even have to have that much faith to produce results, and He used the mustard seed as an example. He said even if we had that tiny amount, it was still enough to affect change in our own lives and manifest what we need or desire. We serve an abundant God, and we have an abundant Savior and Lord in Jesus Christ.

Satan wanted to take Jesus out even as a baby. He did everything he knew to do to discredit Him, to get Him to fall to temptation, and to hurt Him by attacking those Jesus loved—he used the Word itself against Jesus, he tried to get His family to call Him crazy, he tried everything he knew to do, even though he wasn't even sure if Jesus was "the One."

Satan loves it when good people are in pain, suffering, and hurting, and he was thrilled when Jesus was crucified. He thought it was over. But when Jesus rose again, and when He took the keys to hell, death, and the grave, Satan was upset and said that if he'd known, he would have never crucified Him. Why? Because in death, Jesus created our way to eternal life. It was in death that Jesus won. So, don't let death itself fool you. It's not all it's cracked up to be, thanks to Jesus! Abundant life is what He came to give...and it doesn't stop when the grave comes.

JESUS, AN ANTIDOTE FOR A GUILTY CONSCIENCE

It doesn't matter what you've done; if you ask God to forgive you, He uses the blood of Jesus to wash that sin away. Sin just means "missing the mark," and we've all done it and fallen short of the glory of God in some way. There are things people do that they regret for the rest of their lives. Shame clings to them. They can't get over the guilt. But, in Jesus, we have an antidote for a guilty conscience—and even if people try to remind us, God will never do it because He believes His Son's sacrifice is enough to pay the price for *all* sin, and not just the little ones!

Christmas brings a purity of spirit with it, and we are confronted with images that seem like the best and most hopeful ways of living. Images of happy children, peaceful parents, good relationships, and all the sweetest things in life are on display—but for those struggling with guilt or shame, they can barely look at purity without feeling assaulted by the backlash of their own guilty conscience. If that's you, I've got a message for you—you are forgiven. God forgives the worst things, and there is nothing you can do to stop Him from doing it. If you ask for forgiveness and repent with a sincere heart, whatever you did is washed away and it will never be remembered against you anymore. Period.

If we confess our sins to God, He is always going to be faithful and just to forgive us. As far as the east is from the west, that's how far God moves our sins away from us. It doesn't matter how scarlet-red-bad the sin is either! When God washes it away, you are made clean in His sight—white as snow! God has compassion on us, and He understands that we never sin alone. We always have a tempter in Satan, and we are living in a fallen world. But in Christ we find relief from the guilt and shame. In Him, we find no condemnation. Once we repent, He washes those sins away and it's as if they've been thrown into the depths of the sea.

So, ask for forgiveness if something is weighing on your soul—and then let it go. Like you forgive others, forgive yourself. Like God forgives you, forgive yourself. Then, realize the truth: You will have more mercy on others and God just may use you to help someone in the area that you've been forgiven. It's amazing how that works sometimes in life! God turns the bad around and gives you the grace to help another walking in the shoes you used to wear.

The Holy Spirit is a Comforter and a Corrector, and you don't have to worry about sin very much if you stick close to Him—crucify your flesh daily, not just Sunday, and you won't fulfill the lusts of the flesh. It's a daily journey, a daily practice, and a turnaround that He can help you accomplish.

Jesus came to forgive. He came to give mercy and grace. He's a friend Who sticks closer than a brother—and He's the antidote for a guilty conscience. Even in Heaven, He works to "fix" things. If you blow it, the Holy Spirit will tap you on the inside and you will know where you went wrong. That's conviction of sin, but it's not condemnation. That's the Holy Spirit giving you an opportunity to turn to Him, ask for forgiveness, and go the other way. It's not hard. It's just a choice you make. So, why sit in the misery of guilt or try to pay for your sin yourself? You can't do it on your own, and beating yourself up just leads to more misery. You'll be better in the future if you ask for forgiveness and let it go today!

It's the most wonderful time of the year—so let it be that inside of you, too. When you see the manger and you hear the songs, let that purity come through and realize that *you* are made pure and holy in the sight of God the moment you ask for forgiveness and release that junk to God. In Christ, you don't have a merciless master—you have a loving, compassionate, and merciful Savior!

IN JESUS, YOU FIND A REVELATION OF GOD AND YOURSELF

When Christmas is cold here in New Orleans, Louisiana, we sigh relief. I live in a hot-as-Hades part of the world and we never know if we'll be putting sweaters on or wearing shorts to Christmas lunch. But when it's crisp and cold outside, we breathe in that new air and feel the Christmas spirit in the way that we imagine others who live in colder parts do.

When Jesus came, it was just like that in a way—a breath of fresh, cool air came down from Heaven on a cracked and hardened world. In Jesus, we find a revelation of God that is unique and personal and so intimate. When we accept Christ as Savior and Lord, we get to feel God up close and personal—and in that relationship we build, we get a new revelation of ourselves. We find our authenticity in a much greater way. We find a way to stop living in reaction mode to life, and we start to create our life from a place of peace and joy.

Jesus came as a baby, and He won His mother's heart—but it was in His love for humanity and His sacrifice for us all that He won the heart of the world. Time stood still. A cosmic shift occurred. In the spirit realm, angels filled the sky in praise. And when it was all said and done, mankind itself was in an entirely different place. Redemption. Salvation. Victory. New life. New ways of thinking and abundance to be received and lived—spiritually, physically, financially, and in every other way.

In Jesus, we are redeemed. In Jesus, we start again. In Jesus, the switch on this earth was flipped—we now have a way back to God the Father in a pure state, and back to ourselves in the way we were always meant to be.

Once you get a taste of His love, you just never want to go back to living without it. And at Christmas each year, you get the chance to retell the old story and relive that moment in time when God decided to do something really different and really special. The day Jesus was born changed everything, and even though it was over two thousand years ago, it's still fresh and new and full of life-changing power today.

So the next time you are walking around the shops at Christmas, the next time you hear the songs and see a manger with the holy family and all those donkeys, shepherds, scientists, and angels, just remember—*all* of that was for *you*.

God left Heaven for *you*. He came down to earth for *you*. Everything He taught, He taught to give new life and abundant hope and promise to *you*. And when He gave Himself up on the cross, well…that was His whole point from the very beginning. God gave His all and gave His best when He gave Himself for *you*. He did it because He loved you—because He loved the whole world, all of us, including you, just *that* much. He's promised to return—don't forget that very real promise. The end of the story is yet to come!

So, if you want to see Jesus, look into the manger, look into your own heart…and then, look up to the sky! One day you will see Him coming, returning for not only you, but all of us who love Him so much and are looking for His return. And I believe that is *wonderful!*

Salvation Prayer

Jesus is called so many names, but one of my favorites is "the Good Shepherd"—the One Who would leave everything to go and find that one lost sheep. If you don't know Jesus or if you just aren't where you should be and want to come back home to God, would you take a moment to pray this prayer?

All you have to do is reach out to God with a sincere heart and He will reach right back down to you and help you, right where you are. Accepting Christ changes everything, because it changes the heart—it opens the door for a new life in Christ, where all the old things are passed away and everything becomes new. He's listening and loves you, no matter what you've done or how far you've gone, He has made it easy to turn around and just come back where you need to be. Home. Are you ready? This prayer is just a guide, and I encourage you to pray from your heart—remember, you are a spirit and God is going to recreate you from the inside out. That's how He works. It starts in the heart. Would you pray this prayer with me now?

"Lord Jesus, I know You hear me and I want You to know that I need You in my life. Thank You for coming for me, for loving me, and taking me just as I am. I believe You are the Son of God and that You came to save everyone, including me. I ask You to forgive me and help me from the inside now—I know You see my spirit and know my heart, and I accept Your love and sacrifice for me. Thank You for saving me, for bringing me back where I should be, which is with You. I accept You now as my Lord and Savior. I am Yours and You are now mine, and I will never live without You again. I release all my shame and guilt to You, Lord. I give everything I have in my heart over to You to make clean and pure before You. Be with me now, Lord. I accept by faith that You will always, from this day on, be with me. On earth. In Heaven. For the rest of my days and all of eternity. Show me Your ways, Lord. Help me to grow in Your ways so that I can live my best life, starting now. Thank You, Lord! Amen!"

If you prayed this prayer, I want to welcome you into the Family of God. I'm your brother now. You've got brothers and sisters all over this world, and many generations back as well…but you'll meet those in Heaven later! God has so many good kids, and some bad too, but they're all His kids and He loves each one. Find a good church. Read your Bible and listen to messages that inspire you. Go and grow! Remember that God is good, the journey of life is so much better with Him, and your best days are always going to be when you allow His Spirit to lead you. Thank you for giving me the honor of sharing my thoughts and my heart with you through this book. God bless you on your journey!

More About the Author

J esse Duplantis, a best-selling author, has sold more than 1.2 million copies of his books worldwide, with many being translated into multiple languages, as well as Braille editions for the blind. He is the founder of Jesse Duplantis Ministries, located in the Greater New Orleans area of south Louisiana.

In full-time ministry since 1978, with over four decades of evangelistic ministry behind him, Jesse has become known and loved worldwide for his strong, down-to-earth messages, his belief that nothing is impossible with God, and his humorous take on experiences in the believer's life. Generations of believers have been inspired by his messages, and countless numbers have come to know Jesus Christ as Savior through his ministry.

Known for his unflinching, status-quo-breaking messages and his long-standing integrity in ministry, Jesse continues to draw large audiences of believers through television, social media, and meetings held around the world. With a television ministry that spans the globe, Jesse Duplantis continues to be one of the most sought-after

Christian speakers today. With speaking engagements booked years in advance, Jesse Duplantis continues to keep an intense traveling schedule, flying throughout the United States and the world preaching the Gospel of Jesus Christ.

With no booking agents pursuing meetings for him and no set fees imposed upon churches for speaking engagements, Jesse Duplantis chooses his outreach meetings based on the same two criteria he always has: invitations that come in, and prayer over each one. This uncommon way of scheduling means his many followers may find him speaking in some of the largest churches and venues in America and the world, as well as a great many small and growing congregations, too. No church is too big or small for the Holy Spirit, as he says.

Side by side with his wife Cathy, the co-founder and chief of staff of Jesse Duplantis Ministries and the senior pastor of JDM Covenant Church in Destrehan, Louisiana, Jesse continues to fulfill his life's calling by daily taking up the Great Commission of Jesus Christ: *"Go ye into all the world, and preach the Gospel to every creature"* (Mark 16:15).

Through television broadcasts, books, and other ministry products, as well as through evangelistic meetings, the JDM website, the JDM app, social media, and *Voice of the Covenant* magazine, Jesse Duplantis continues to expand his reach while maintaining his roots. Jesus is the center of his life. The salvation of lost people and the growth of believers is the purpose of his ministry. And for both he and his wife, every day is another day to *"Reach People and Change Lives, One Soul at a Time"* with the Gospel of Jesus Christ and the success-producing principles of the Word of God.

Other Books by Jesse Duplantis

Your Everything Is His Anything
Expand Your View of What Prayer and Faith Can Do

Advance in Life
From Revelation to Inspiration to Manifestation

The Big 12
My Personal Confidence-Building Principles for Achieving Total Success

Living at the Top
How to Prosper God's Way and Avoid the Pitfalls of Success

For by IT…FAITH
If You Don't Know What "IT" is, You Won't Have It!

DISTORTION
The Vanity of Genetically Altered Christianity

The Everyday Visionary
Focus Your Thoughts, Change Your Life

What in Hell Do You Want?

Wanting a God You Can Talk To

Jambalaya for the Soul
Humorous Stories and Cajun Recipes from the Bayou

Breaking the Power of Natural Law
Finding Freedom in the Presence of God

God Is Not Enough, He's Too Much!
How God's Abundant Nature Can Revolutionize Your Life

Heaven: Close Encounters of the God Kind

The Ministry of Cheerfulness

OTHER CONTENT:

Other ministry resources by Jesse Duplantis are
available through www.jdm.org,
the JDM App, and *TotalJDM.org*
(a subscription service of Jesse Duplantis Ministries).

To contact Jesse Duplantis Ministries
with prayer requests, praise reports, or comments, or to schedule
Jesse Duplantis at your church, conference, or seminar,
please contact us at:

JESSE DUPLANTIS MINISTRIES

PO Box 1089
Destrehan, LA 70047
985-764-2000
www.jdm.org

WE ALSO INVITE YOU TO
CONNECT WITH US ON SOCIAL MEDIA:

- Facebook: /JesseDuplantisMinistries
- Twitter: @jesse_duplantis
- Instagram: @jesseduplantisministries
- YouTube: /jesseduplantismin
- Pinterest: /JesseDuplantisMinistries

The Harrison House Vision

Proclaiming the truth and the power
of the Gospel of Jesus Christ with excellence.
Challenging Christians
to live victoriously,
grow spiritually,
know God intimately.